Praise for *Talk Less, Say More*

"*Talk Less, Say More* is packed with powerful advice to get your points across and make things happen in today's time-pressed world. Connie's forward-thinking, actionable communication shortcuts can elevate anyone's game."

—Bruce Carbonari, Chairman & CEO,
Fortune Brands

"Connie Dieken is a true communication virtuoso and a genuine phenomenon. She is on a mission to elevate our ability to communicate. *Talk Less Say More* should be required reading for all leaders and emerging leaders. It can instantly transform the way people respond to you, giving you the power to deliver brief, clear messages that influence the world.

—Robert Johnson, Managing Counsel,
McDonald's Corporation

"Connie Dieken's three-step strategy is a smart, practical guide for business leaders and others who want to create a high-performance culture. It's an important, powerful book on how to master communication in the 21st Century."

—Tom Swidarski, President & CEO,
Diebold

"*Talk Less, Say More* has become an integral part of our sales training program. In today's manufacturing environment, our sales engineers must be able to quickly gain mind share of our customers, deliver the appropriate messages, and win new business. *Talk Less, Say More* provides the communication tools critical for success."

—Dana Fritz, Manager, Global Sales Training,
Rockwell Automation

"*Talk Less, Say More* is the answer to become an effective communicator. Connie's principles can be employed immediately to improve both your personal and business interactions."

——Terry Bauer, Corporate Director of
Sales Execution, Reinhart FoodService

"Thanks to Connie's communication expertise, she makes it easy for anyone to transform from a good communicator to an excellent one. Her three simple principles are based on real-world experiences and demonstrate the power of a strong communicator."

——David Lingafelter, President,
Moen Incorporated

TALK LESS,
SAY MORE

3 Habits *to* Influence Others *and* Make Things Happen

CONNIE
DIEKEN

WILEY
John Wiley & Sons, Inc.

To the two most influential people in my life,
Spencer and Ali

Contents

Introduction
Connect-**Convey-Convince**®

Face-to-face communication skills are plummeting in the twenty-first century. What does it take to be an influential communicator in today's information-overload, attention-deficit, distraction-driven world? Do you have to morph into a super-human communicator to keep people tuned in to your ideas when you're face-to-face?

No, when it comes to communicating influentially in our fast-paced, Twitter-happy society, less is more.

Now More Than Ever, Less Is More

You can become a high performance communicator if you simply get into the practice of using three habits in the right order. This simple shift in how you get your points across will create an enormous change in how people respond to you, whether you're talking to an audience of one or one thousand.

Forget the endless communication techniques that you've heard about over the years. All of those

1

techniques actually boil down to just three skills: Connect-Convey-Convince®. I first discovered this high performance secret when I was a television news anchor and talk show host with access to communication masters such as former president Bill Clinton, sex guru Dr. Ruth Westheimer, and General Electric CEO Jack Welch. I studied skilled communicators as they influenced our television viewers, studio audiences, and television production staff, which sparked my decade of high performance communication research and, ultimately, this book.

Tired of Struggling to Get Your Points Across?

This book is brief but meaty by design. It will teach you how to use these three principles to win positive responses in a world of short attention spans, even from the most difficult people in your life and those who are the most distracted and impatient. Suddenly, people will pay attention to you, understand you clearly, and commit to action.

Consider how you currently approach communication. In our crazy busy world, words flow from your mouth or fingertips. You explain, request, plead, sugarcoat, apologize, question, and/or demand. All in a quest to make things happen. Sometimes your words inspire action. However more often, they don't. Even worse, your attempts spark subsequent back-and-forth exchanges to clarify what you really want. Time is wasted, mix-ups occur, and opportunities are squandered.

In your rush to meet today's overwhelming demands, you're probably using tech tools to dodge and deflect. Case in point: how often do you do these things?

- Check caller ID, think, "Not you, not now," and send the caller to voice mail jail, playing digital dodgeball?
- Check voice mail and e-mail simultaneously?
- Grow impatient with long-winded callers and zap their messages in midsentence?
- Return people's calls, hoping they're not there, only to be disappointed when they pick up the phone and you actually have to talk to them?
- Talk to someone in person when your cell phone rings . . . and you answer it, leaving someone hanging?
- *Communi-fake,* pretending to be on your phone to avoid talking to someone in person?

The question is, How often are others doing this to *you?* Every one of us has our own "buttons" that get pushed, leading to negative results, including tune-out. People push your buttons. You push theirs, too, even when you don't intend to.

It's time to press the right three buttons for results in today's fast-paced world to keep people tuned in and raise your ratings.

Becoming an influential communicator is the solution. This sequence of habits—**Connect-Convey-Convince**®—will help you grab attention, gain complete clarity, and sway others to

It's Time to Engage, Gain Clarity and Commitment

make things happen. It will help you successfully influence even the busiest people.

The strategy is simple, and yet it creates profound differences in how others respond to you. Suddenly, you'll become a high performance communicator who keeps people tuned in and wins positive results.

Let's get started maximizing success by minimizing words.

HABIT 1: CONNECT

MANAGING ATTENTION

**Give People What They Want
and Value So They'll Tune In**

10 SIGNS
YOU MAY BE A WEAK CONNECTOR

Do You Do This?

1 You have trouble getting people to listen to you, pay attention to your ideas, or return phone calls or e-mails.

ISSUE: CONNECTING ESSENTIALS

FIND HELP: page 11

2 You're impatient, easily distracted, or often multitask while communicating.

ISSUE: STAY IN THEIR MOMENT—STAY RIGHT HERE, RIGHT NOW

FIND HELP: page 19

3 You don't listen well, interrupt frequently, dominate discussions, or start most conversations with what matters most to you.

ISSUE: STAY IN THEIR MOMENT—LISTEN FOR INTENT

FIND HELP: page 21

Are You a Weak Connector?

4 You're preoccupied with how others may be judging you.

ISSUE: STAY IN THEIR MOMENT—AVOID CODE RED

FIND HELP: page 23

5 You frequently ramble, take too long to get to the point, or have been told that you're dull or boring.

ISSUE: FRONTLOAD—NAIL THE BIG IDEA

FIND HELP: page 31

6 You automatically use the same method of communication to reach everyone—the method that *you* prefer.

ISSUE: FRONTLOAD—CHOOSE THEIR PREFERRED METHOD OF COMMUNICATION (PMOC)

FIND HELP: page 34

7 You're not good at reading people's body language, or you have trouble reading between the lines of what they say.

ISSUE: FRONTLOAD—DEFUSE DEFENSIVENESS

FIND HELP: page 37

8 You're often judgmental or critical of others in public.

ISSUE: GOLDILOCKS CANDOR—DON'T DEMORALIZE

FIND HELP: page 47

9 You sugarcoat, sidestep, or hold back to avoid conflict or criticism.

ISSUE: GOLDILOCKS CANDOR—DON'T SUGARCOAT

FIND HELP: page 49

10 People don't share honest, timely feedback with you.

ISSUE: GOLDILOCKS CANDOR—CREATE A CANDID CULTURE

FIND HELP: page 50

Why Connect?
Attention Management

Does this sound familiar? You're sharing an idea in a meeting when a sinking feeling washes over you that *no one is paying attention*. A quick scan of the room confirms it. Some people are distractedly thumbing BlackBerry devices under the table. Others have dashed out to take phone calls. Still others are fidgeting with text messages. The few who are not ignoring you are so impatient that they cut you off and talk over you.

That's what happened to David, an emerging leader at a global consumer product company. It was happening in everyday conversations, but it really upset him when it occurred during a presentation.

David was puzzled, thinking what went wrong? He'd spent endless hours preparing for his big moment—gathering information, confirming facts, and painstakingly creating dozens of difficult slides. He had immersed himself in preparation.

Engage or Be Ignored

Yet, when he stood in front of his audience to deliver the message, he lost them at hello.

David experienced the most common communication breakdown facing business professionals today: he *failed to connect*. He didn't manage his audience's attention. As a result, he had no chance to *convey* his message so they'd clearly understand it, or *convince* others to make decisions and take action.

Chances are this has happened to you today, in a conversation, a phone call that wasn't returned, or even an ignored e-mail. In this chapter, you'll discover the first step for communicating at your highest performance level in a distracted, attention-deficit world. You'll learn how to capture people's hearts and minds so you don't lose their attention or drive them to distraction.

Make It a Habit

Have you noticed that some people are natural connectors? They seem to attract attention like magnets. Why? The world's top communicators make connecting a habit.

The difference between the masters and the rest of us is that they've learned to make connecting *automatic*—they do it every time, with every person. They make engaging people and managing their attention a priority.

Perhaps you have the gift—this power to draw attention. If not, don't worry. Connecting is a learnable skill. It's not like singing ability. You can learn to be an A-list connector even if you've spent your whole life skipping this step and ending up ignored or tuned out.

Connecting is the ability to engage and manage people's attention in today's busy world. It's changed profoundly. It's no longer enough to make contact. Now you must give people *what they want and value* in order to earn their attention, or they'll tune you out. Connecting used to be a "nice to have" competence, but it's now a make-or-break skill. That's because there's been a monumental power shift in communication. The listeners now hold the power. It's as if they hold the remote control and you're just one of many TV channels. They have options, so if you want to be Must-See TV, you must connect smartly.

The people you're communicating with can zap you at any moment with their internal remotes, lured away by more appealing distractions such as e-mail, text messages, cell phone calls, or Web surfing. People have become so impatient in our fast–faster–fastest world that they don't even wait for you to finish a sentence—they cut you off and talk right over you.

Today's Make-or-Break Skill

Our attention-deficit world also encourages people to disconnect from in-person conversations:

- Have you ever been talking with someone when their cell phone rings and they choose to answer it and leave you hanging?

- Has the person in the next cubicle ever shot you an e-mail instead of walking over to talk to you?

- Are people keeping you at arm's length with e-mail and text messages instead of returning calls or talking face-to-face?

Blame the lure of instant gratification. Think about it: we're now conditioned to get what we want, pronto. For example, there's GPS, speed dating, instant messaging, quick weight loss surgery, spray tans, ten-minute whitening strips—the list is endless. You don't even have to pay professional dues anymore, with shortcut shows like *American Idol* around to catapult you to the top. We've become a shortcut society.

That means you have to win people over in a hurry as attention spans shrink. It's vital to connect with people on their terms. So how do you do this? Simple: *Give people what they want and value right up front.* That's my definition of smart connecting: Give people what they want and value so you keep their attention.

Biggest Blunders: Self-Absorption and Aimless Schmoozing

Think of a time when you failed to engage someone. Why did you fail to connect? There are countless reasons. Among them, perhaps you:

- Took too long to get to the point
- Chose the wrong method
- Didn't focus on the person
- Failed to grasp their true resistance
- Misjudged what they wanted or valued
- Lost your head and came across badly
- Sugarcoated a subject or demoralized someone
- Weren't specific enough
- Used a one-size-fits-all approach

All of these scenarios cause tune-out in today's short-attention-span, self-absorbed society. What's the solution? Give people what they want and value, quickly. If you simply zero in on what matters most to your audience, they'll reward you by paying attention. Like Tom Cruise in the movie *Jerry Maguire*, you'll have them at hello.

Now that you realize connecting is critical in our instant-gratification society, it's time to start putting this attention-grabbing rule to work so you can advance toward *conveying* important information and *convincing* people to act. The first section of the book will focus on smart connecting strategies and techniques that you can start using today to manage the attention of your audience, enabling you to perform at your highest level and make your ratings soar.

2

Stay in Their Moment
Be Fully Present

Staying in their moment means fully focusing on the needs of the people with whom you're communicating. It means first managing your own attention in order to win other people's interest. This triggers a positive gut reaction that engages people and keeps their attention focused on you and your message. Use this strategy and you'll attract, not *dis*tract.

Linda, an up-and-coming corporate executive, learned to *stay in their moment* after her self-absorption led to disastrous results. It happened at 7:30 on a Monday morning. As Linda was checking e-mail and reviewing her schedule of wall-to-wall meetings, her phone rang. It was the CEO of another organization. "I've heard great things about you and I'd like to explore having you join our leadership team," he said. However, as the conversation unfolded, the CEO didn't like what he was hearing.

Fully Focus on Their Needs

17

Linda came across as distracted and rushed. She interrupted him and talked over him. The CEO got the impression that Linda was self-absorbed and too unfocused to be an effective leader on his executive team. He quickly crossed her name off his short list of prospects.

Linda learned her lesson. What specifically did she change about her communication approach in order to stay in the moment? She stopped reading e-mail when she was on the telephone and disciplined herself to focus on the conversation at hand.

John, a sales executive at a large consumer goods company, saved his biggest account by staying in their moment. In a meeting with a longtime client, John was pitching a product line when he sensed that something was amiss. He couldn't put his finger on it, but he was smart enough to stop pitching and start focusing on his client's needs. He asked, "Randy, I have a feeling that something's on your mind. How can I help?" By asking the right question and then listening carefully, John unearthed what his client didn't volunteer: Randy was considering defecting to John's competitor, who was actively wooing him. John had been taking his relationship with Randy for granted and failing to connect in ways that were meaningful to Randy. Staying in the moment at the meeting allowed John to give the client the attention he valued and hold on to a major account.

My questions for you are: Are your connection skills getting rusty? Has high-tech connectivity eroded your personal connectivity? Are you inadvertently coming across as self-absorbed, distracted, or rushed and losing opportunities as a result?

Following are three tactics to help you stay in their moment to ensure that people stay engaged.

Did you know that one of the most influential speeches in history occurred because the speaker "stayed in their moment?" Dr. Martin Luther King's *I Have a Dream* speech is an example of this technique in action. When Dr. King finished his prepared speech on the steps of the Lincoln Memorial on a hot August day in 1963, he scanned the faces of his massive audience and realized they needed *more*. That was when Dr. King launched into "*I Have a Dream.*" It wasn't planned. His words stirred the nation because he appended "*I Have a Dream,*" which he had recently delivered from his church pulpit, to the end of his talk. By staying in their moment, Dr. King stayed fully connected with his audience and transfixed a nation.

You can do this too. You can be right here, right now with any audience. Use the antennae you've sprouted during your lifetime to stay fluid and give people what they need. Scan for signals to key in on your listeners' vibes—both the good and bad ones. You'll know when to insert an addendum, when to shorten your talk, and when to actively listen.

STAY IN THEIR
MOMENT
TACTIC 1
Be Right Here, Right Now

TIPS   *Here are a few pointers for being right here, right now:*

Show respect. If you duck your head into someone's office and they appear engrossed in their work, demonstrate respect and earn their future attention with words like, "I see that you're very busy right now. Is there a better time for me to come back to discuss this?"

Don't race ahead. Fight the urge to jump in because your mind has raced ahead and you think you know how they're going to finish their sentence. Commit to hearing the other person out completely. You may miss their real point if you cut them off.

Aim for the heart, not the head. Concentrate on people's feelings first. The heart trumps the head, so get real with the power of emotional appeal and you'll earn people's attention.

Don't be a drifter. Do you sometimes drift in and out, as a rambler yammers on and on? Prevent drifting by focusing on the big picture of their message instead of their incessant words.

Focus on people, not electronics. If you're presenting material from a laptop or standing in front of a screen, don't focus your attention on the slides. No matter how impressive your slides are, it's more important to watch your audience to see how they're reacting.

Watch for eye movement. If people raise their eyebrows or their eyes dart nervously, it's a clear signal that you've touched a nerve, or perhaps slipped on a banana peel.

Observe their lips. The lips are among the most emotional parts of the body. Drooping or pursed lips are usually an unvoiced sign of disappointment or disagreement.

Notice the tongue. Ever see someone stick the tip of their tongue through their closed lips? It's a negative signal. It generally means they disagree with or don't like what you're saying.

Adapt your style. It's up to you to communicate in the receiver's style, rather than expecting them to adapt to yours. If you're dealing with an analytical, nuts-and-bolts person, give them the facts they crave. With a drama queen, make certain to address the emotional needs.

STAY IN THEIR MOMENT TACTIC 2
Listen for Intent

Quick: Recall a day in your life when every single word, every single sentence, came out exactly as you intended. You were flawless as a communicator, effortlessly spewing words that resonated with and inspired others. No one misconstrued a word you said.

Can't think of a day like that? Whew—then you're like every other human being on the face of the earth.

What you say is often not what you mean. Your messages frequently morph somewhere between your brain and your mouth. That's why it's dangerous to be stuck on the exact words that *others* utter, since their intentions trump their words, too. What's truly important is the emotion behind the words. Staying in their moment means listening with discipline to interpret their true intention—what they really meant.

So how do we put this strategy of listening for intent to work?

Listen for repetition. This provides a clue to the speaker's hot-button issues. People repeat what they really want and value—especially if they feel they're not being heard.

Take note of emphasis. When you hear a word stressed with added *oomph*, take the hint. That particular word holds significance to the speaker. Ask a question like, "Could you tell me more about that?" to clarify their intention.

Rephrase as a question. Double-check your understanding to avoid potential confusion. Ensure clarity and gain respect by saying, "Let me see if I've got this right. Are you saying . . . ?"

Don't take negative questions personally. Some people may voice concerns because they sincerely want to dig deeper. Stay open. Honest questions are a sign of interest in your message and a chance to show your expertise.

Don't be hijacked in meetings. Sometimes the concerns of a single individual can irritate everyone else in the group. Don't spend too much time answering one person who peppers you with questions (unless it's your boss or another executive). That person's intent is often to look good.

Have you ever had an "out-of-body experience" in a stressful situation? Ever lost your head when your emotions kicked in? Had trouble thinking on your feet? Some people feel paralyzed in high-profile communications; others strut like peacocks. These are both what I call Code Red situations, which can damage your career.

Photo Credit: Department of Homeland Security

What do I mean by Code Red? Consider the Homeland Security Advisory System, that color-coded chart that warns the public about the possibility of a terrorist attack. The peak level, indicating a severe risk of attack, is red. It's generally called "Code Red."

STAY IN THEIR MOMENT TACTIC 3
Avoid Code Red

I believe many of us create our own personal Code Red situations during important communications that prevent us from staying in the moment. They're the extremes of fight or flight and are absolutely damaging. Unfortunately, we aren't always aware of our Code Red situations until it's too late.

Kelly nearly crashed her career this way. She's a director at a global consumer products corporation and the only woman who meets regularly with their executive team. She's also a self-professed Type A personality who has trouble containing her emotions.

Kelly used to get overly emotional to the point of tears when she felt her contributions were being attacked. The executive team was starting to discount her and take her less seriously as a result.

How did she learn to control her emotions and change her destiny? Kelly printed a small copy of the color-coded Homeland Security chart and taped it inside her pad folio. When she finds herself getting out of control, she focuses on the chart, which reminds her of her elevated state and helps her calm down and stay in the moment.

The antidote to losing control is to focus outwardly on your audience instead of focusing inwardly on your own needs and nuances. This will help you stay connected to others instead of damaging your career.

TIPS   *Here are some tips to avoid Code Red when you're feeling off-balance:*

Slow the moving train. Your mind runs at warp speed when you're in front of an important audience. You overanalyze or censor each idea. Out-of-body experiences are controllable if you simply slow yourself down. You'll process information more efficiently and come across as natural and likable.

Follow the law of inverse proportions. The more inflammatory the question, the more calmly your answer should be delivered. Don't be drawn into argumentative baiting—you'll look and sound defensive.

Self-correct. Mistakes are an inevitable part of high-profile communications. If you slip up, don't let embarrassment cause you to sidestep the issue as if it didn't happen—you'll appear out of touch or arrogant. Instead, acknowledge your error and correct it on the spot.

Make midcourse changes. When you pick up on clues that your audience is upset or tuning out, stay flexible and adapt. It could mean altering your agenda or changing the topic to something more relevant. Top communicators are responsive to others' feedback.

Don't defend the indefensible. A wise CEO of a multibillion-dollar corporation says it infuriates him when people aren't open to others' criticism of their ideas. Don't be overly rigid in defending your stance or you'll alienate others and miss opportunities to make your great idea even better.

Don't grandstand. State your opinion with passion and then listen carefully to the feedback. Don't get caught up in the "I have the floor" game. The goal is to initiate dialogue—not to launch into a lecture others could interpret as a diatribe.

FIVE TIPS TO STAY CONNECTED WITH DIFFICULT PEOPLE

There's a challenging person in your life who is very difficult to communicate with. You know who he or she is. That person is likely self-absorbed with a grandiose sense of entitlement, impulsiveness, or explosive anger. Here are some tips to manage conversations with that person:

1. **Offer options to difficult people.** Beneath their bluster, difficult people often fear being left out of the loop. They crave control. Better to stay in their moment and offer them options. This can help them feel in control and respected. It also prevents nasty hissy fits.

Staying in the Moment with Difficult People

2. **Anxious people often hear what they expect to hear.** We're primed to hear the news we fear the most. Some may interpret your message as bad news even when it's not. To prevent gossip and ensure clarity, ask difficult people to repeat your message in their own words.

3. **Don't sidestep.** If you're confronted, don't hide. Ask for time to give the person's comment respectful thought and then schedule a time to address it. You will appear confident, empathetic, and forward thinking by handling the confrontation sincerely.

4. **Politely redirect windbags.** A naysayer cuts you off as you're talking. He's off-topic. A simple, "That's a good idea, but it's not our topic right now," can do the trick. Your polite redirect can save your meeting. Other participants will thank you for saving them from the pontificator.

5. **Apologize swiftly and sincerely.** Don't let bad feelings fester. If you've made a mistake, express your regret to mend the relationship and then focus your energy on a solution.

....

FIVE TIPS TO ACCEPT CRITICISM LIKE THE MASTERS

1. **Keep the criticizer's intent in mind.** Good bosses and clients offer criticism because they want you to perform at the top of your game. Their feedback is intended to improve performance, not diminish you as a person.

2. **Ask for clarification.** The best approach to criticism is to listen carefully and then ask for clarification so that you completely understand their point of view.

3. **Incorporate what you learn.** Winners know there's at least a small grain of truth in most criticism. Step back and adjust your performance based on the feedback you've received.

4. **Fight the urge to jump in.** Allow the person to voice their tirade completely before you respond. Listen and wait. Exercise your patience gene. If you jump in too early to defend yourself, the difficult person will toss more verbal grenades.

5. **Take their emotional temperature.** What's the emotion behind the criticizer's words? Do they want to help or are they just tossing verbal grenades in order to feel superior? If it's the latter, respond respectfully with "Thank you for the feedback" and let it go.

....

FIVE TIPS TO CRITIQUE WITHOUT DEFLATING OTHERS

1. **Make your point without making an enemy.** Smart communicators remember two things: people and performance. Both matter when delivering your critique. Don't sacrifice one for the other or people will duck, dodge, or deflect.

2. **Don't dodge the truth.** Leaders can't avoid criticizing direct reports. It's part of your job.

However, you can avoid making a mess by handling criticism with smart sensitivity. If a direct report's performance problem is taking an immediate, irreversible toll on others, don't put off the conversation.

3. **Minimize fallout.** You've heard the saying "Praise in public, criticize in private," right? You'll minimize emotional fallout by keeping critical appraisals confidential.

4. **Use the sandwich technique.** Preface your criticism with a positive statement about their performance or character. End upbeat, as well. The critique goes in the middle.

5. **Prepare for a meltdown.** Some people over-react, no matter how sensitive your approach. Keep them focused on how to improve their performance in order to minimize their knee-jerk reactions.

3

Frontload
First Things Fast

Frontloading is my term for quickly nailing what's relevant to your listener, so they immediately grasp what's in it for them and don't tune you out. It's the antidote to rambling.

You're in the office, sleeves rolled up, and ready to face the day. With the wind at your back, you accomplish task after task. Then, screeeech . . . halt. In walks a rambler. He secretes his poison: "Do you have a sec? Um, you know, I've been thinking. On Wednesday, when you said . . . or was it Tuesday? I think it was Tuesday, but maybe it was even Thursday. Blah, blah, blah . . . " On and on he blathers, jumping from one tangent to another. Before he showed up, you were Peyton Manning driving for a touchdown, but you just got sacked.

Ramblers force you to wade through their long-winded, tedious digressions before they get to their point—if they actually have one. Your mind

Quickly Nail What's Relevant to the Listener

wanders as they jabber away. You're bored silly and just want to be put out of your misery.

The question is, are you that person? Do you ramble or otherwise belabor points, triggering others to tune you out? If so, frontloading is the solution.

The Solution to Rambling

Mark, a vice president of a global manufacturer, was a deliberate perfectionist and an accidental rambler. His failure to deliver succinct messages turned his executive team off. They felt he was hijacking their meetings with his endless belaboring of points. Even worse, when his points failed to sway the team, he circled back around and started repeating himself. He mistakenly thought repetition and additional details would pile-drive his messages home.

The team was frustrated. They knew Mark was a brilliant man who executed strategies flawlessly, but they hated to wade through his flawed communicating.

An amazing thing happened once Mark learned to frontload. His newly concise messages led to instant success. He became far more influential and started getting his projects and budgets approved quickly. If you think Mark is delighted with the results of frontloading, you should talk to his peers. They're overjoyed that he's no longer hijacking their meetings by rambling.

How to Frontload a Message

Simply deliver the most relevant part of your message *first*. The key is to make certain your message is relevant to your listener and pared down to its core. To practice, think of a message you need to deliver to a specific audience. Consider what this audience wants and values most. Now take out a small sticky note, 3" x 4" or smaller. Write a brief headline that marries the essence of your message to the audience's most pressing need or deepest value. That's the part of the message that you deliver first. Think of it as a customized headline. Frontloading grabs people's attention and keeps them tuned in.

Following are three tactics to help you connect by frontloading, along with several tips to integrate frontloading into your life.

FRONTLOADING TACTIC 1

Nail the Big Idea

One of the most common frontloading failures happens because you dive into details before sharing the big picture. The audience can't grasp the relevance because they don't see what it means to them.

You must first make sure everyone is clear on your big idea, your vision, before you get down into the weeds with the details.

You have the curse of knowledge, so chances are you do this every day. You're so close to your topic that you forget that others aren't privy to information you take for granted. You assume everyone knows what you do. However, they don't.

Robert, the new CEO of a major consumer product company, made this mistake as he presided over his first annual meeting as chief executive. His industry was in free fall in a weak economy. His audience, the top one hundred company executives, was jittery. The theme of the meeting was leadership. Did Robert open the meeting with how he planned to lead the company through turbulent times? No. With what the audience members needed to do to lead their business units? No again. Robert led his first annual meeting as chief executive with "housekeeping" details, such as break times, the agenda, and who else would be speaking. He inadvertently skipped the big picture about his vision for the company's future and missed an opportunity to inspire trust in his leadership as the new CEO.

Don't skip the big picture or you'll lose people at hello. Nail the big idea and others will stay connected to you. You'll equip them with the context to execute the details in your plan.

TIPS   *Here are a few tips to help you nail the big idea:*

Don't bury the lead. Capture and summarize the critical essence of your message quickly. Make sure everyone clearly understands the big idea before you dive into the details. Think newspaper headline—that's the essence. Otherwise, people won't have the context to understand and/or execute the details.

First words are sticky. The first words out of your mouth get stuck in your listener's mind. To the listener, they define your purpose and signal what they should act upon—positively or negatively. Make these words work for you.

Think John Madden. Don't be a play-by-play announcer, be a color commentator. Share insights and analysis—what you make of the facts—instead of merely dispensing factoids. This way, you'll be perceived as the go-to subject expert. Let's say you're at a team meeting trying to win project approval. Share how your project will improve the team's overall performance and what it's going to take to win big.

Give it the *TV Guide* test. Can you boil your message down to a few pithy sentences? That's how TV listings work. They offer a quick synopsis of a lengthy program, which is all that people often want in our supersaturated society. Save the lengthy versions for people who opt in and request more details.

Picture an accordion. Great communicators understand that there are long versions and short versions of everything. When your audience lacks the time or patience to digest details, think accordion. Squeeze the accordion bellows together and make your long story short. Keep the long-winded details in your back pocket, because you may need to pull the bellows out to answer their questions.

Tease like a TV producer. Need to cover multiple topics? Take the *Today Show* as an example of how to cover multiple topics without losing the attention of listeners who aren't interested in all of the subjects. The *Today Show* begins with a short preview of what's coming up later in the program, which in TV lingo is called a tease. You can tease, too, if you have several topics to cover.

Put a number on it. People magically remember numbers. They like the structure. They even count along with you in their heads. This is a good strategy if you have several points and you want people to tag along. If you have three points, announce it at the beginning: "I have three things I want to discuss with you. Number one . . . "

Deep-six the laundry list approach. Reciting a list of what's happened since your last meeting doesn't drive your team forward. It slips you into reverse and bores people silly. Instead, frontload with success stories, the progress you've made, and the most actionable items.

FRONTLOADING
TACTIC 2
Choose Their PMOC

Another way of frontloading to capture attention is choosing the right method. This involves both the mechanical method and your style approach. We'll cover them both, but let's start with the mechanical.

You have your Preferred Method of Communication (PMOC). Which device do you robotically reach for to deliver outgoing messages—your phone or your keyboard? That's your go-to method; you probably favor that same method to receive communications.

I'm asking you to stop automatically choosing your favorite method and shift to your receiver's preference. *Their* PMOC trumps yours because they control how soon they will respond to you— if they respond at all. Choose their PMOC and you'll increase your odds of getting a quicker, more positive response. Before you deliver your next message ask yourself, "What method does the other person prefer?" That's the right method.

Andy, a sales rep, was hot on the trail of Larry, a potential customer, but lost him because he didn't know Larry's PMOC. Andy heard that Larry was ready to close a deal with a competitor, and he was sure he could win Larry over if he could just reach him before the deal was signed. Andy peppered Larry with voice messages. What Andy didn't know was that Larry hated voice mail and didn't bother checking it often. Instead, Larry was an e-mail addict and carried his BlackBerry everywhere. When Larry finally listened to Andy's voice messages, he'd already closed the deal with the other suitor. Which method did he use? His favorite format: e-mail.

Sharon learned the hard way that firing off an e-mail was not the right way to thank the vice president who interviewed her. The vice president chose another equally qualified applicant, in part because the other applicant took the time to send a handwritten thank-you note. Sharon lost the job by not noticing that the vice president valued a personal approach. If she'd scanned his desk during the interview, she would have noticed many handwritten notes.

Choosing their PMOC goes beyond selecting e-mail or voice mail. For example, Amazon.com and iTunes are masters at staying in your moment. Both keep track of your buying history and suggest other products in the same genre. They earn many additional sales by tapping into your buying habits.

PMOC n.
Preferred Method of Communication

It also applies to how people prefer to receive messages—with a light touch or a heavy hand. Best-selling Author and Pastor Joel Osteen is a master at choosing the right touch. Osteen's nondenominational Texas church is the nation's largest congregation. Its 30,000 members meet at the Compaq Center, the former home of the Houston Rockets. Osteen's sermons are featured on television and in sold-out arenas around the country. How does Joel Osteen begin each sermon? He begins with a joke. Osteen is a gifted storyteller and uses spiritually connected jokes to make his audience laugh. Think of his jokes as sorbet. They cleanse the palate and prime people to receive the rest of his message.

TIPS *Here are some tips to help you choose the right PMOC:*

What's their magnet? Notice which communication method your recipient is drawn toward. Observe which one they choose most often or which method they respond to most quickly. I recommend that you simply ask people for their preference. Record this in your address book and make it your default method to reach them.

Deliver as peer-to-peer instead of teacher-to-student. Nothing turns people off faster than feeling as if they're being lectured. A heavy hand often leads to automatic resistance, or worse yet, a knee-jerk "no." The exception to this rule is reprimands, when the person should understand that they're receiving an order.

Boost your personal bandwidth. What's your default talking style? Do you interrupt a lot, sugarcoat, demand, lecture, and/or apologize? Make it a point to be aware of your go-to communication style and switch it up in order to connect with other people's styles. A one-size-fits-all approach drives people crazy.

Aim for the heart, not the head. Light a fire under people by concentrating on their feelings first. The heart trumps the head. Get real with the power of emotional appeal and you'll motivate people to connect with you and commit to action.

Forget perfect—strive to be relatable. Which do you prefer—genuine or phony? Of course, you want others to keep it real, so you should, too. Stop worrying about being flawless and an amazing transformation will happen. People will be drawn to you and relate to you. They'll root for you and keep listening.

You're Diana Ross; your slides are the Supremes. Have you ever been trapped in a presentation where the presenter loaded his slides with tons of text and read it aloud to you? It was awful, wasn't it? Don't let too much text trigger disengagement. The bottom line is that Power-Point slides should not be a teleprompter. Your expertise is the star—your slides are the back-up singers.

If you're communicating with a person who's angry, upset, or resistant, you can use frontloading to defuse their defensiveness.

FRONTLOAD
TACTIC 3
**Defuse
Defensiveness**

Face it—some people are a real pain to communicate with. Do you have difficult people in your life? Isn't it a challenge to connect with them and get your message across? They resist you, twist your words, cut you off, take things the wrong way. Wouldn't it be great to reduce their resistance so they'd hear you out?

Learning this skill helped Greg prevent expensive turnover in his department. Greg is a director in a large corporation. Mike is one of his new account managers. Greg and Mike are polar opposites. Greg is a thoughtful, deliberate leader. Mike is an alpha male, loud and boisterous, interrupts everyone, and has what Greg calls a pinball brain that jumps to conclusions before thinking things through. However, Mike is also very talented and tenacious, which makes him valuable. Mike was driving everyone around him crazy and resisting guidance to tone it down, which landed him on probation after six months with the company.

Finally, Greg got through to him. How? He tapped into what Mike valued. "Mike, would you like the opportunity not only to get off of probation, but to advance your career?" he asked, which was positively received by Mike. Greg continued, "I see tremendous potential in you. You're tenacious and contribute solid ideas. I admire those qualities." Mike felt great and his resistance dropped. "But did you realize you have a career-limiting habit?"

Greg finally got through. Once Mike's knee-jerk resistance was lowered, Greg was able to get to the root of Mike's interpersonal problems. Turns out, Mike was boisterous because he lacked industry knowledge and tried to cover it up by being loud and dogmatic. He agreed to be aware of the impact his behavior had on those around him. Once Greg frontloaded with positive remarks, he was able to lower Mike's resistance, which saved Mike's career . . . and Greg's sanity.

Maybe you've been the resistant one. Have you ever waited on the telephone to be connected to support for a product for a long time? Finally, after an hour of listening to bad music with periodic recordings about how much the company allegedly values your business, a representative comes on the line. "Customer service. My name is . . . " You jump in and let the representative have it. You complain about how long you waited and then start unleashing about what's wrong with their product.

How would you handle it if you were on the receiving end of steady tirades? (Even if they are tirades of your own making because you placed people on hold so long.) Verizon Wireless has found a way to reduce the resistance. They allow callers to vent their pent-up frustration first, and then they frontload with reassuring words like "I can definitely help you with that." This assurance soothes the angry customers and earns trust.

Resistance isn't limited to difficult people, of course. Sometimes you have to present difficult or unwanted news that is met with opposition from even the nicest people. How do you deliver bad news without triggering the kind of resistance that causes people to stop listening?

TIPS   *Here are some tips to stay connected by reducing resistance:*

Make your point without making an enemy.
Smart communicators remember to focus on two things: people and performance. Both matter when you deliver bad news. Don't sacrifice the person's feelings by focusing solely on their performance, or they will shift to defensive mode. They'll stop listening to you because they're busy defending themselves, saying, "Yeah, but . . . "

Express respect to defuse hostility.
If the other person is deeply entrenched in their corner or hostile, start your communication with cooperative words like "I see your point" or "I understand how you could get that impression." It will lower their resistance far more than starting with fighting words that they will resist.

Positive wins, so radiate confident energy.
Radiate likeability and enthusiasm, even with difficult people. Stay positive to fight back against the energy suckers. Listen actively and convey positive interest and optimism whenever possible.

Keep smiling.
It's hard to be angry with someone who's giving you a genuine smile. Just keep it real and don't try to pass off a smirk as a smile.

Watch your tone.
Do you inadvertently use a know-it-all tone? A high-and-mighty tone ticks people off and makes them want to push your buttons and say no to you. Share unwelcome news in a firm but friendly voice.

Consider your state of mind.
Before you deliver negative news, examine your intentions.

Are you feeling angry? Betrayed? If so, cool down before you lose your head. Don't let your own state of mind cause the other person to resist you.

Don't be a smug mug. There's a delicate balance between self-assured and arrogant. Don't slip into the latter. Think warmth and likeability.

Give them options. Don't start by telling a difficult person what to do. This causes some people to automatically resist you since they feel out of control. Instead, give them options and ask them to choose the one that's best for them.

Make them the hero. Have you noticed that some difficult people toss verbal grenades when other people are the center of attention? They value being recognized as champions. To stay connected with a narcissist, make them a key part of the story. Their ears perk up and resistance is lowered when they're recognized.

Let them take ownership. Ever notice that some people don't like an idea unless they think it's their own? Let them take credit. You're in a tug of war, so drop the rope and allow the narcissist to take ownership of the idea.

4

Goldilocks Candor
Get Ready to Rumble

Does this sound familiar? You're in a meeting with Ms. Snippy and Mr. Ever Rude. As their turf battle heats up, the meeting swiftly descends into cheap shots, sarcastic barbs, and one-upsmanship. You feel as if you're watching a cable television shout fest. The attack artists try to drag you into the battle. Do you candidly respond that they're being world-class jerks? Do you dish up a little sugarcoating? Do you calmly but firmly respond that it's time for other voices to be heard?

What about this one: A work friend is talented, but he comes across as arrogant. He's gaining a reputation as a self-possessed, brash, inflexible guy. Do you tell him he's earning a reputation as a jerk? Do you do nothing? Do you privately explain that his behavior is career limiting and offer to help him recalibrate?

Finally, have you ever been in this position? It's late Friday afternoon in conference room 3-A, where your project team has gathered for the final meeting of the week. A peer presents an idea that you think is lame. You've been swamped, you're in a bad mood, and you want to get this meeting over with so you can finish your work. Do you channel your inner Simon Cowell, rip into her proposal so everyone will see the holes, and dismiss the idea? Do you bite your tongue, withholding your insights on the subject in order to get the meeting over with? Alternatively, do you offer to speak with her offline after the meeting to share your experiences?

The Right Level of Candor Is Crucial to Stay Connected

Choosing the right level of candor is crucial to keeping people connected and listening to you. It's critical to your success to get this right. Without connecting, you can't successfully convey or convince. The wrong level of candor can lead to defensiveness, hurt feelings, withholding, or poor performance—none of which helps you get people to listen so you gain understanding and convince them to act.

Have you ever been on the receiving end of poor candor? Has someone demoralized you by lobbing verbal grenades? Have you ever been led astray because someone sugarcoated the truth? The candor gap is growing in today's fast-paced world. There are three types of misguided attempts:

1. Some people are lobbing borderline-cruel criticisms in the workplace.

2. Others are sugarcoating in order to avoid conflict and be liked.

3. Still others are retreating into passive-aggressive behaviors, being nice to your face but unleashing harsh comments behind your back.

Today's abundance of communication tools, including e-mail, cell phones, text messages, blogging, Twitter, and social networking on sites such as Facebook and LinkedIn, are giving people plenty of opportunities to stay connected and use candor.

Are you using smart candor? If you're getting it right, these things are happening:

- People share their ideas directly and honestly with you, without fearing they'll look stupid.

- They share their thoughts without fearing payback or repercussions.

- They don't feel disregarded or brushed off when they contribute.

- They don't get the wrong impression that you approve of their ideas when you really don't.

- They weigh their options openly and respectfully, with everyone allowed to voice their opinions.

Need some help? Let's look to Goldilocks for how to get candor right.

How to Use Goldilocks Candor

What is smart candor? Think of it as a Goldilocks test: not too hard, not too soft—it's just right.

Smart candor works wonders because it demonstrates integrity, which keeps people connected to you. They'll reward you by continuing to listen.

....

The purpose of workplace candor is to improve performance. Used judiciously, candor encourages contributions, boosts productivity, and leads to a positive culture.

....

Smart Candor Improves Performance and Contributions

Organizations without candor pay the price—sometimes disastrously. Consider what happened at NASA, a workplace that, until recently, discouraged candor by dismissing the concerns of underlings. In February 2003, the space shuttle *Columbia* disintegrated during reentry into the earth's atmosphere. All seven astronauts died.

Engineers on the project had tried to warn higher-ranking officials that the mission was doomed; attempting to point out problems with the fuel-tank insulation, but officials dismissed their concern. Turns out, the brushed-off engineers were right all along. The insulation broke off and punched *Columbia*'s wing, damaging the thermal tile protection system that caused the catastrophe.

Did the culture change? Not yet, it took another high-profile issue to instigate a more candid atmosphere at NASA. This one involved drunken astronauts. In 2007, a health panel disclosed that at least twice, astronauts had been cleared to fly despite being intoxicated. Flight doctors and other astronauts had warned officials that some astronauts were drinking heavily before flying, but their warnings were ignored. The flight surgeons said they felt demoralized and were less likely to report concerns in the future.

Why did officials ignore the warnings? Simple, they were under pressure to launch on time, and they suppressed unwelcome news. It's costly to delay a launch, both financially and politically, so they weren't open to news that could lead to delays. They zapped bad news like bugs on neon.

NASA has since taken steps to remove the communication barriers that made people feel too afraid to speak up. It has moved toward a more open, candid culture that empowers anyone to raise concerns.

What's your candor gap? Creating a more candid culture is a game-changer. Following are the top three gaps and tactics to close them.

CANDOR TACTIC 1
Don't Demoralize

Here are a few tips to ensure you don't use the type of candor that, in Goldilocks terms, is too hard:

TIPS

Offer solutions, not hostility. Be very specific in your criticism. Contribute to a solution rather than aiming to seize control or look smarter than others. Instead of bullying or blaming scapegoats, focus on things that can be changed.

Don't be the faultfinder. Impulsive faultfinding and criticizing others' ideas doesn't make you appear discerning. Excessive criticism creates a distrustful culture and earns you a reputation as a negative person and character assassin. Don't do it and don't tolerate it.

Be tolerant of different viewpoints. Do you give the impression that it's your way or the highway? This pushes people away. Don't force your opinion on others. Draw people out instead of shutting them down. Be tolerant so people will continue to make contributions.

State and listen. State your opinion with passion—and then listen carefully to the feedback. The goal is to initiate candid conversations, not to launch into diatribes that hurt others and reflect poorly on you.

Don't be careless. Resist the impulse to shoot off your mouth or make a joke at someone else's expense. Think through the implications of whom you could offend or hurt. Pounding on every gaffe causes people to lock up and withhold information.

Crank the volume down a notch. Have you ever heard someone slip into grandstanding mode when they criticize? Did they talk louder? Tone it down so it's not overly harsh. Don't use an overly aggressive tone to display your toughness.

Choose a positive tone. This is where people separate the good intentions from the ugly ones. A haughty, know-it-all tone ticks people off and makes them want to disregard your input. Use a firm but friendly voice. Think candid, not abrasive.

Contain the outbursts. Do you rant? Are you prone to explosions? That doesn't register in the office. Don't lose your cool. You'll alienate people who otherwise would be in your corner. Stay calm and people will listen to you.

Avoid EUI (e-mailing under the influence). Whether you're mad or flippant, keep a cool head before hitting the send button. Think how many people would see your words if your e-mail was forwarded to the masses. Today, more than ever, words matter.

Do you have a habit of holding back for fear that people won't like you? Do you sidestep so you don't have to deliver unwelcome news?

In sensitive or sticky situations, people will often paint a picture rosier than reality in order to avoid an awkward conversation. Often, we'd rather perjure ourselves than have an uncomfortable discussion.

Sugarcoating and hiding bad news are damaging to both your organization and your well-being. When you hold back information, it merely delays outcomes and often makes them worse when the person learns the real truth. It's better to face the issues and get them on the table so they can be resolved faster.

Here are a few tips to ensure that you don't sugarcoat:

Understand why you sugarcoat. Are you a people-pleaser? Do you want to be liked? Identify your motivation. Awareness is the first step to solving the issue.

CANDOR TACTIC 2
Don't Sugarcoat

TIPS

Introduce candor by asking a question. Try starting with a question like "Have you thought about . . . ?"

Stop dooming others. You can doom others by giving them bad input. You'll help others use better judgment if you arm them with accurate information, even if it's not what they want to hear.

Don't be selfish. While you may be trying to spare another person's feelings, sugarcoating is also selfish. It's a superficial way to appear more appealing.

Don't be a yes-person. Executives are often surrounded by yes-people who filter out bad news. This helps them convince themselves that strategies are working, even when they aren't. Dare to be the person who tells the truth.

CANDOR TACTIC 3
Create a Candid Culture

How do you introduce candor if your culture is prone to grenade lobbing or sidestepping? It starts with leadership.

Leaders should demonstrate smart candor and reward those who get their ideas on the table to help improve performance. Once a team starts talking directly and honestly, the culture will shift and candor will become more natural.

TIPS   *Here are some tips to get it right in your organization:*

Invite candor. Define what candor means to you and why it's important. Let others know you value straight shooters because they make the business more idea-rich, cut costs by eliminating mind-numbing meetings, and benefit everyone, every day.

Model candor. If leaders express themselves candidly and thoughtfully, this behavior will travel throughout the organization, raising expectations and performance levels.

Reward candor. When others are upfront with you, praise it—publicly. Spread success stories and reward candor with your thanks.

Admit mistakes. Don't pretend you're bullet-proof. Capitalize on your errors—articulate the lessons learned, internalize them, share them—and move on. Advise others to do the same.

Reach the best answer. The objective of candor is to ensure that your team arrives at the best possible answer, not to let individuals display power and fire missiles. Make the best answer your North Star.

Avoid fighting words. "You never" and "you always" are combative words. They cause people to get defensive. The recipients are so busy defending themselves that they shut down and disconnect.

Ask withholders for input. If you notice people being quiet, draw them out. Be inclusive. Ask for their opinions and their help to understand something better.

Live your values. Are integrity and respect among your top values? Live them when you communicate and you'll cultivate productivity.

Not on your watch. If you observe others dishing out demoralizing words or sugarcoating, you must address it. Otherwise, you're giving them permission to make it a habit.

There's a distinct line between bluntness and demoralization. Excessive criticism leaves people deflated and afraid to deal with you again. It leads to a cover-your-butt mentality that keeps great ideas off the table. This doesn't mean that you can't speak your mind: just dole it out without scorched-earth criticism that leaves emotional scars.

A candid culture keeps people connected, gets more people in the game, and generates speed to improve business performance.

You need people who will give you direct and timely feedback and vice versa. Constructive feedback shouldn't demoralize—it should empower. If you have direct reports, don't wait until the year-end performance review to dump bad news. People are typically on the defensive during reviews, and not as open to coaching. If you haven't been honest during the year, it will lead to an unpleasant surprise and they will feel blindsided, which will undermine trust.

If people fall short of expectations, make a meaningful effort to tell them earlier rather than later. They will trust you and gain confidence that you're working together toward the same goal.

....

HOW TO TAKE CRITICISM

It's hard to be on the receiving end of criticism, isn't it? Consider how top performers on television shows like *American Idol* accept even the cruelest feedback. Here are some lessons learned to help you respond at the top of your game:

Ask for clarification. The best approach is to listen carefully and ask for clarification so you fully understand their point of view.

Resist the temptation to become defensive. Defensive reactions make your critics even more determined to search for issues in the future and zap you even harder.

Listen for emotion. Do the critics really want to help your performance, or do they merely enjoy feeling superior? If it's the latter, merely respond respectfully with "thank you."

Incorporate what you've learned. The winning contestants on TV shows know there's at least a small grain of truth in most criticism and so should you. Step back and adjust your performance based on the feedback you've received.

Connect Review and Action Plan

Engage to Manage Attention

Connecting Prevents Tune-Out

In today's fast-paced world, people want to know what is important to them—otherwise they tune out. In order to connect, you must engage and manage people's attention right away by starting your communications with what's most relevant to the listener.

As the first of the 3 Habits, the ability to connect lays a foundation for the other Habits to build upon. You have to connect with people before you can successfully convey and convince them.

STRATEGY 1
Stay in Their Moment

Staying in their moment means tapping into other people's needs and values. How good are you at truly staying in other people's moments and tuning into their needs and values? Are you focused, listening intently, and avoiding distractions? On the other hand, are you caught up in your own world and missing signals?

What Could I Improve?

❑ TACTIC 1: BE RIGHT HERE, RIGHT NOW

❑ TACTIC 2: LISTEN FOR INTENT

❑ TACTIC 3: AVOID CODE RED

❑ OTHER _____

My Action Plan:

_____

_____

_____

STRATEGY 2
Frontload

Frontloading is the antidote to rambling. To frontload, quickly pinpoint what's relevant to your listener and communicate what matters most to them first so they don't tune out. They'll immediately grasp what's in it for them and stay connected to you.

What Could I Improve?

❑ TACTIC 1: NAIL THE BIG IDEA

❑ TACTIC 2: CHOOSE THEIR PMOC

❑ TACTIC 3: DEFUSE DEFENSIVENESS

❑ OTHER _____

My Action Plan:

_____

_____

_____

STRATEGY 3
Goldilocks Candor

The right level of candor is critical to provide and receive feedback. Smart candor improves performance and contributions. Goldilocks candor means not too hard, not too soft, it's just right.

What Could I Improve?

❏   TACTIC 1: DON'T DEMORALIZE

❏   TACTIC 2: DON'T SUGARCOAT

❏   TACTIC 3: CREATE A CANDID CULTURE

❏   OTHER _____

My Action Plan:

_____

_____

_____

My Current Approach

People tune me in when I . . .

_____

_____

People tune me out when I . . .

_____

_____

Why have I approached connecting in these ways? . . .

_____

_____

Next Step

Now that you've managed people's attention by connecting effectively, it's time to move on to conveying, which means managing what they know.

HABIT 2: CONVEY

MANAGING INFORMATION

Use Portion Control to Get Your Points Across with Clarity, Not Confusion

10 SIGNS
YOU MAY BE A WEAK CONVEYOR
(And Where to Turn to Conquer Them)

1 You tend to confuse people or make things sound more complicated than they really are.

ISSUE: CONVEYING ESSENTIALS

FIND HELP: page 65

2 You use additional words to convey ideas instead of using visuals

ISSUE: THE EYES TRUMP THE EARS—SHOW CONTRAST

FIND HELP: page 74

3 Your PowerPoint slides are packed with text, text, and more text.

ISSUE: THE EYES TRUMP THE EARS—RETHINK POWERPOINT

FIND HELP: page 76

Are You a Weak Conveyor?

4 You haven't discovered the right social media tools to convey your messages.

ISSUE: THE EYES TRUMP THE EARS—LINK IT, MOVE IT, USE SOCIAL MEDIA

FIND HELP: page 79

5 You give people numerous options to choose from—and they often seem stuck.

ISSUE: TALK IN TRIPLETS—PRELOAD THREE CHOICES

FIND HELP: page 85

6 You're fact-driven and tend to dive into details, or you pile on numerous points in an effort to be comprehensive and cover all the bases.

ISSUE: TALK IN TRIPLETS—THINK NARROW AND DEEP

FIND HELP: page 86

7 You save the best for last.

ISSUE: TALK IN TRIPLETS—DESIRED CHOICE FIRST

FIND HELP: page 89

8 It's unusual for you to share success stories or reveal positive anecdotes.

ISSUE: TELL STORIES—SUCCESS STORIES

FIND HELP: page 93

9 When you tell stories, people get lost because your stories tend to be drawn-out or convoluted.

ISSUE: TELL STORIES—THINK SIMPLE AND SPRY

FIND HELP: page 95

10 You sound stiff when you deliver stories or presentations.

Turn the Page for Help

ISSUE: TELL STORIES—DELIVER WITH PLANNED SPONTANEITY

FIND HELP: page 97

5

Why Convey?
Information Management

Using the strategies you discovered in the previous chapters, you've already connected successfully, earning the person's attention. Why lose them by conveying information in a sloppy manner? Conveying successfully leads to clear understanding, which will allow you to convince them later on.

Let's start with this premise: Smart conveying is radically different in today's information-laden society than it was just a few years ago. Social scientists say we're buried beneath an avalanche of information ten thousand times bigger than what an earlier generation had to deal with.

Your world is full of *communiclutter*, which you need to conquer in order to convey successfully. What's that? It's my term for communication overload—when you're bombarded with endless streams of communication 24/7, making it difficult to focus and process all of the short-burst,

Create Clarity, Not Information Overload with Messages

incoming electronic information. Sound familiar? Your inbox is cluttered, your cell phone is cluttered, your desk is cluttered—and as a result, your mind is cluttered. You need shortcuts to process and understand it all.

Com-mu-ni-clut-ter® n. Information Overload Caused by Being Bombarded

In our new world, communiclutter is inescapable. What we can't prevent, we must embrace—and manage. Just as you manage your incoming communications, you should also manage your outgoing communications to cut through other people's information overload and win results. That's information management.

Yours will be the message that cuts to its essence and gets understood, despite the fact that you started with a staggering amount of information. Your message will say in one page what others say in ten. Your message will be smartly distilled and conveyed with impact, an exercise in mental refinement that allows your words to be clearly understood. You'll take smart shortcuts. You'll use portion control to create accurate take-aways and ensure that others understand you. You won't overwhelm people with data dumping.

We now ignore the vast majority of information that comes our way. The key to smart conveying is to understand that information is *not* knowledge. Information has to be processed first before we understand it and then it becomes knowledge. This is a challenge because we're all deprived of the time to absorb, process, and understand information, let alone integrate it into our lives.

Let's try this on for size. You're at a convention. After the opening session, you follow the masses to the closest breakout room—the topic looks on point. You spot an open seat, squeeze into a middle row, and are set to learn.

The presenter gets started. He's a mild-mannered fellow who fumbles through slide after slide of text-laden PowerPoint, unloading way too much information in a single bound. You're bogged down, dazed, and confused. What do you learn? Nothing.

Alternatively, how about this: Have you ever received a voice message so longwinded that the caller gets disconnected and has to call back to leave an addendum? What happens as a result? You waste plenty of time in frustrating back-and-forth calls until you're able to pinpoint what she actually needs.

Finally, has this happened to you? Your inbox pings and it's a prolonged e-mail data dump from a colleague. It's way too time-consuming and con-voluted to handle now, and besides, it's a cover-your-butt e-mail, sent to a dozen people. Repulsed, you quickly close it and move on. You intend to revisit it later, but you never do. Later, you learn there was an action item for you buried near the bottom. Oops, you didn't read down that far.

These are examples of how people squander opportunities by making conveying blunders. The question is, are you guilty of overloading others, too? Are you confusing people with messages that are too long, complex, and difficult—if not impossible—to follow?

Biggest Blunder: Data Dumping

Maybe you're a credible content nut who values finding and delivering lots of information. You may feel like you're cheating people if you don't share every last fact. However, are you grasping the downside? You may be oblivious to how much time you're taking and how much you're bogging people down with information.

The key to conveying in today's fast-paced world is portion control. Portion control is a smarter way to convey because it forces you to manage your messages so that others can process your information accurately. It leads to clarity.

Are You Conveying or Confusing?

Data dumping is undisciplined communicating; a form of overcommunicating that leads to confusion, misunderstandings, and wasted time. You bog people down and they resist— and resent it.

Using the smart conveying skills in the three chapters that follow, you'll discover techniques that use portion control to create clarity, not confusion.

Overloaded e-mails, voice mails, presentations, and in-person conversations are incredibly frustrating, especially now that we're all bombarded with hundreds of daily communications. Like a dieter counting calories, you need to relearn what a proper serving size really is. Once you get into the habit of using portion control, you'll help your listeners absorb and understand even the most complicated messages.

How do you apply portion control when you convey? What if you have a really complicated message? How do you know what to leave in and what to leave out? Read on to learn simple strategies to convey successfully.

6

The Eyes Trump
the Ears
Use the Dominant Sense

When I was a young TV reporter, one of my first plum assignments was covering the Kentucky Derby for NBC stations. Imagine my excitement, approaching Churchill Downs in search of human-interest stories for the week leading up to the Derby.

One day, my assignment was to feature the Anheuser-Busch Clydesdales. There I was, tiny Connie, surrounded by hulking horses. Suddenly, my cheerful chatting was cut short when, with cameras rolling, a two-thousand-pound, plow-pulling, purebred Clydesdale began to *eat my hair*—on television! Neophyte reporter that I was, out of embarrassment and shock, I carried on with my report as if nothing was happening. (To be fair to the horse, my dry, lacquered locks must have looked like lunch to a creature that consumes fifty pounds of hay each day.)

A Shortcut to Clarity

My ridiculous televised hair scare taught me a valuable lesson beyond the need to lay off the lacquer: The eyes trump the ears. As you can imagine, no one heard a word I was saying—I could have announced the cure for cancer and it wouldn't have sunk in. My audience was too caught up in a visual distraction worthy of the Derby slogan, "The most exciting two minutes in sports."

What does "the eyes trump the ears" mean to you when you're conveying a message in the office or the boardroom?

Brad, a financial fund advisor, learned the power of this strategy in the workplace when he failed to use it. He inadvertently created chaos instead of clarity.

Brad was invited to a school board meeting to deliver good news—the school was the recipient of an $80,000 gift from an alumnus who had passed away. However, it wasn't that simple. The windfall was left in a named fund that Brad would manage, split into two separate funds. The school could access 6 percent of each fund per year and was permitted to spend the funds, divided equally, in two areas that the deceased had designated: scholarships and grounds upkeep. Further, if the school didn't use the money in either of the two funds, the money would roll over and grow annually.

Don't Create Chaos

Confused? So was Brad's audience. Right away, Brad could see the commotion he'd caused as he tried to talk them through the complicated process. Some board members got stuck on the $80,000 figure—in their excitement, they started chattering away about buying a new roof. Others were puzzled by the 6 percent explanation, trying to do the math and wrap their heads around that number, or was it two numbers? Still others were baffled by the multiple fund designations.

The more Brad talked, the more muddled the group became.

What was missing? What could Brad have done differently to prevent the confusion? In hindsight, the answer was crystal-clear. If he had shared a simple visual, the board members wouldn't have gotten dazed and confused.

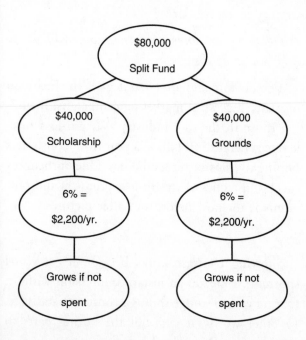

Vision is the most dominant human sense. Your brain processes visuals up to ten times faster than mere words, according to research in both educational theory and cognitive psychology. Memory soars when you see visuals instead of mere text.

Visual learning is a shortcut that creates clarity because it helps people organize and analyze information, as well as integrate new knowledge quickly.

Any time you can show rather than tell you'll reduce the risk that the receiver will misunderstand, misconstrue, or mangle your message. You'll get the results you want, faster.

Why Do The Eyes Trump the Ears?

How can you use the "eyes trump the ears" strategy to create clarity?

Following are three tactics with plenty of tips to help you apply them.

The "before and after" strategy is the lifeblood of many successful marketing campaigns, including those in the diet industry. Weight-loss marketers generate $30 billion a year from consumers hoping to transform their bodies. One of the most successful tactics of weight-loss products and programs is to show before and after pictures.

EYES TRUMP EARS TACTIC 1
Show Contrast

Showing contrast works because it's a visual shortcut. It creates an instant impression without forcing you to trudge through confusing statistics. In other words, it cuts out the boring parts to create a visually induced belief.

Photo credit: Quick Weight Loss Centers

You can use the contrast approach successfully in many ways, including:

- Simple graphs
- Clear-cut charts
- Demonstrations
- Props
- Side-by-side comparisons

Using contrast, you can demonstrate growth or market dominance, or even exploit a competitor's weakness.

Contrast Proves Results

Famed defense attorney Johnnie Cochran successfully used this technique to argue to a jury that his client, O.J. Simpson, was framed for the murder of his ex-wife. As he launched into his closing argument, Cochran pulled on a pair of gloves similar to those the prosecution used to link Simpson to the murder scene. He reminded the jurors of the apparent difficulty Simpson had getting the gloves to fit during the trial. Remember the phrase that goes with the photo?

Photo Credit: REUTERS/Vince Bucci/pool

"If the glove doesn't fit," Mr. Cochran said, "you must acquit." By using the "eyes trump the ears" technique to convey his message, Cochran was able to convince the Simpson jurors to let his client go. As a well-trained attorney, Cochran knew that people respond most positively to what they see, not what they hear.

EYES TRUMP
EARS TACTIC 2
**Rethink
PowerPoint**

PowerPoint is a blessing and a curse. While it makes producing presentations a snap, the program allows you to take two equally poor paths that violate the "eyes trump the ears" principle:

Too much text. This leads to excruciatingly boring presentations. Who has the patience for tedium? You'll miss your chance for success if you force people to sit through slide after dreary slide of the same old predictable bullet point format.

This approach is wordy, dull, and unfocused. It's so old school that you might as well use an overhead projector with transparencies if you slip into this mode.

The Case For Too Much Text on PowerPoint Slides

- Don't you hate it when people create too much text and then read it out loud to you?
- It's bullet after bullet of boring fact because you haven't been punished enough today.
- These "facts" aren't even relevant, but they fill the space and make the author feel smart.
- If you're really lucky, you'll witness the words warp and fly onto the screen like a superhero on steroids.
- Did I mention that putting too much text on slides is worse than having no slides at all?

See what I mean? Reading wordy text from slides to your audience undermines the purpose of your communication. It's monotonous, which causes tune-out and inhibits understanding. It also undermines your credibility by making you appear to lack the confidence or knowledge to share information without a pseudo-Teleprompter.

Too many jazzy graphics. You may be tempted to go clip-art crazy, but slides that are overloaded with every bell and whistle in your software's arsenal also undermine your message. This approach creates empty garbage that lacks detail, intellectual analysis, or even any real substance at all. You've heard of all sizzle and no steak.

Don't Undermine Your Credibility

Even PowerPoint's creators Robert Gaskins and Dennis Austin agreed that you could veer seriously off course trying to dress up dimwit ideas. They were interviewed by the *Wall Street Journal* for PowerPoint's twentieth anniversary in 2007. "It's just like the printing press," said Austin. "It enabled all sorts of garbage to be printed."

Indeed, when you open the software program, you're tempted to favor format over content and overdo it. However, that abomination is controllable. Remember that clarity is achieved through simplicity and portion control.

So how should you use PowerPoint to take advantage of the "eyes trump the ears" technique?

TIPS   *Here are a few tips:*

You're the first visual. Don't let the slides eclipse your talent. Also, quiet your mannerisms and other distractions. When your body language contradicts your words, guess which signal wins?

Right, in the eyes of an audience, your body language negates your words.

Fight presentation bloat. Think highlight reel when you create a slide deck so you don't create too many slides. Too much of anything dilutes its power and muddies your message.

Cut the noise. Noise is anything on a slide that distracts from the clarity of your message. Minimize the noise by eliminating the excess. Think simple and clean.

Use visual shortcuts. Most speakers load their slides with text and charts. Do the opposite. Paint a picture of clarity by using more photos, video clips, and other punchy visuals. Better to be short on bullets and big on visuals.

Guide their glances. When you're showing a slide full of numbers, highlight the ones that you want the audience to zero in on. That way, focusing on the wrong number won't distract them and lead to chaos and misunderstandings.

In the pre-Internet days, you had limited access to stimulating visual resources. Now they're easy to gain access to, so why not use the information you find or plant there to your advantage. Social media can create visual perceptions in a flash.

Here are a few resources that can help you tap into the "eyes trump the ears" strategy in our new world:

- **YouTube. Grab your popcorn: We're living in the YouTube era.**

EYES TRUMP
EARS TACTIC 3
Link It, Move It—Use the Social Media

Presidential candidates now face questions directly from voters. A scorned wife uses the format to humiliate her estranged husband. Recruiters are trolling the site for video resumes, and police are posting clips from security cameras to snag criminals. Soon, using YouTube videos to get your points across will be as ubiquitous as iPods and smart phones.

If you haven't thought about a YouTube presence yet, it's time to embrace it. Otherwise, someone else could beat you to the punch and make a smash hit of you, with images that are beyond your control. You could be forced to deal with a game-changing gotcha moment.

- **Other social media like Facebook, LinkedIn, Twitter, blogs, and video podcasts.**

    These are visual platforms to chronicle your existence and update your status. They're new ways to advance your cause and raise your profile. Social sites have grown at astonishing rates because they link people together visually.

Key to Using Visuals Successfully in the Social Media?

Have you seen Facebook's social graph? It's a mathematical construct that maps the connections between people. On a social graph, you're a node radiating links to the people you know. What does this mean to you? Once you upload a photo or other profile information, Facebook organizes it visually to everyone via the social graph.

The appeal of social sites is both obvious and subtle. They are an Internet within the Internet. In this opt-in world, people have to consent to have contact with you or even see others on the network. If you annoy people or don't appeal to them visually, they can drop you off the grid. You will cease to exist.

Here are a few tips: **TIPS**

Post clear, simple ideas. Think "Evolution of Dance" or other Internet hits. Don't overload with too many ideas. Your job is to convey the essence of your message, not everything you know.

Once you upload it, it's there forever. Remember that before you hit the send button. Have another set of eyes check your visuals to ensure that they convey the intended message.

Make it a quickie. Who surfs the Internet for comprehension? Most people are distracted when they're online. Either they're at work, where they're not supposed to be surfing, or they're at home, where Fido beckons. Brevity is king to conquer short attention spans.

Don't let your wardrobe overwhelm your message. Unless you're a fashion designer or movie star, keep it simple. Choose dull finishes over shiny ones, avoid excessive makeup, and wear a natural, understated hairstyle. Don't distract people with your appearance.

Convey warmth if you're on camera. There's a delicate balance between looking self-assured and looking arrogant. Pull up your cheek muscles, warm your eyes as if you're looking at an adorable puppy, and convey likeability.

Don't slip into business-speak or industry jargon. Don't fall prey to your own curse of knowledge. Social media are available to the masses—don't ruin your chance to convey clearly by speaking a secret language, unless you're only preaching to the choir.

7

Talk in Triplets
Tap into the Trilogy

Did you know that your mind craves information in multiples of three? Three is the world's most powerful number for receiving information, which means it's a secret shortcut to convey messages powerfully. If you want to save time and effort in helping people understand your messages, structure them in variations of threes.

Not sure how to pull this off? Let's see how messages are communicated in threes in all areas of your life. In the chart are just a few of the triplet combinations that participants in my business communication workshops have come up with.

The World's Most Powerful Number

Education
- 3 Rs: Reading, 'Riting, 'Rithmetic
- Elementary, Middle, High School
- Bachelor's, Master's, Ph.D.

Sports
- NBA, MLB, NHL, NFL, PGA, WWE
- Horse racing: Triple Crown
- Baseball: 3 strikes, you're out; 3 outs/inning

Entertainment
- Network acronyms: ABC, NBC, CBS, FOX, PBS, CNN, HBO
- 3 Blind Mice, 3 Stooges, 3 Musketeers, 3 Little Pigs
- Lights, Camera, Action!

Sciences
- Solid, liquid, gas
- Animal, vegetable, mineral
- Fats: saturated, monounsaturated, polyunsaturated

Personal Safety
- Stop, drop, and roll
- Stop, look, and listen
- 9-1-1

Law
- Legal trilogy: Voir dire, opening, summation
- The truth, the whole truth, nothing but the truth
- Attorney, client, witness

Business
- CEO, COO, CFO, CIO, CMO
- GNP (Gross National Product)
- Big Three automakers

Basics
- Day, month, year
- Area codes
- Red, white, and blue

Government
- Executive, legislative, and judicial branches
- IRS (Internal Revenue Service)
- FBI (Federal Bureau of Investigation)

Colloquialisms
- Hop, skip, and a jump
- Beg, borrow, or steal
- Eat, drink, and be merry

Blah, Blah, Blah. Yada, Yada, Yada.

The list goes on and on. Blah, blah, blah. Yada, yada, yada. Get the point? Triplets are so ingrained in your daily life that you probably aren't even aware of the pattern. However, subconsciously you're comfortable with three of anything. It just feels right.

Too much of a good thing can lead to confusion, as the leader of a national sales force learned. He was frustrated that his regional managers weren't grasping his priorities for the year. I asked him to rattle off the priorities for me; he whipped open his laptop and double-clicked a document with a list of 20 priorities. Twenty!

As I stared him down, the light bulb clicked on in his head. He had too many priorities. No portion control, no understanding, no action. Once he funneled the list down into three top priorities, the bewilderment shrunk and his market share soared.

How can you use this potent trilogy of persuasion to your advantage? Following are three (of course) tactics.

TRIPLETS
TACTIC 1
Preload Three Choices

The concept is simple, but powerful. If you want someone to make a choice without delay, preload three choices. In other words, give them three ready-made options.

This technique speeds up the dynamics of decision making. Since the conscious mind loves three, the receiver will feel satisfied that they have plenty of alternatives, but they won't feel so overwhelmed that they delay or resist making a choice altogether.

Many retailers understand this concept. You'll see this technique in action successfully in commerce. For example, Amazon.com displays three books per row. It's not too much and not too little: it's just right. The iTunes Store displays three hot new albums in its home page header, and if you've shopped for an Apple computer, you'll notice that the online store displays three choices of computer configurations at a time.

If you've ever bought anything from an infomercial, the rule of three may have reeled you in. Producers of these programs typically use the "three easy payments" method to make products seem irresistibly tempting.

I've seen the power of this technique personally. I once cohosted a television program for a high-end retail client for a product that cost about $500. In test markets, consumers responded positively to the product and its promotion, but most declined to buy because they said the price was too steep. What did our producer do? She had my cohost rerecord the payment portion of the program, changing it from full price to "three easy payments." Bingo! Magically, resistance dropped and the product started selling.

TRIPLETS TACTIC 2
Think Narrow and Deep

The rule of three works equally well when presenting any type of information that you want people to act upon, beyond just making choices. The narrow and deep formula works in any communication format to avert confusion. Presenting ideas in a narrow and deep way, as opposed to wide and shallow, will cement your ideas and prevent them from getting lost in communiclutter.

How to do it? In e-mails, you'll achieve glance-and-go clarity by presenting ideas or info-bits in quick bullets. By separating information into bite-sized pieces, you'll avoid the monotony of paragraphs and help the information stand out.

For example, scheduling a meeting could look like this:

- Tuesday, July 19
- 1:00–2:30 P.M.
- Conference room 3-A

In a phone call that involves multiple topics, compress them into three topics, start with the words, "Three things," and then state the three. Why? The mind latches on to numbers like a bulldog snatches a steak. Announcing a number in advance creates an alert mind.

In presentations, narrow and deep is the most powerful and compelling structure. That means three key points with supporting subpoints. Why? Because it combines hard data with gentle simplicity and it's organized in the way the mind likes to receive information—in threes.

See the following figure for what I call the accordion structure in formal presentations:

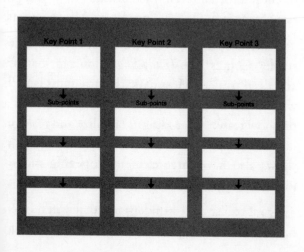

The Accordion Structure

When pressed for time—let's say you're relegated to talk at the end of a meeting and a colleague spills over into your time (big surprise, eh?)—simply lop off the bottom subpoints. That way, you'll still get to the most important points and use everyone's time efficiently. This sure beats only getting through one point and kicking yourself afterwards that you didn't cover other important material.

Conversely, if you find yourself faced with extra time in a presentation, you simply add more depth to your three points. Perhaps you share a success story, add an activity, or provide more tactics. Use the narrow and deep formula and you're ready for anything that comes your way.

You probably didn't realize it, but you see information presented in threes in a narrow and deep format on television every day. Think of the most basic television show: your local news. How many components do they have? Three: news, weather, and sports. The show's producers add or chop information in each of these three categories based upon the day's needs. It's a fluid format.

Moreover, when you watch television news staples such as *The Today Show*, look for narrow and deep triplets. Most days, the programs launch with a quick preview of three stories. It's called a preshow tease: Three ideas to tantalize and reel you in, then they go narrow and deep. Late-night TV shows also have three elements: opening monologue, desk guests, and stand-up entertainers.

I'm a realist, and I understand that you'll often have more than just three options to present.

However, consider condensing them to three in today's overwhelming world. Three strikes and you're in!

A question I am asked many times about triplets is "What order do I put things in?" In response, I ask, "Which one do you want them to choose?" The key is to put your desired choice first.

TRIPLETS TACTIC 3
Desired Choice First

I learned this powerful key when I hosted a series of training videos for the world's most profitable bedding company. The videos coached sales floor staff to successfully sell high-end mattresses in the stores.

If you've ever shopped for a mattress with a salesperson guiding you on the showroom floor, you know the trick. Which mattress did they ask you to lie down on first? The most expensive or the least? Of course, it was the priciest.

Why? Because product research says that most of us, when faced head-on with the most luxurious choice, will have a hard time resisting it. We don't want to settle for less once we've sampled the best.

This tip works not only for selling consumer products, but also in everyday communications. The lesson is this: When presenting ideas or choices in threes, don't just go linear. Frontload with your desired choice. (Remember frontloading from the connecting section?) Your next preferred choice goes in the last position for a strong finish. Your least favorite choice gets buried in the middle.

However, what if a person is chronically indecisive and still can't make a choice from three options? Let's say you give a friend three selections for fast-food lunch spots—McDonald's, Wendy's, and Taco Bell—but "I don't know" is their wishy-washy mantra. Here's the trick: ask them to eliminate one. Works like a charm. If all else fails, once you get them down to two, flip a coin!

8

Tell Stories
Gain Longer Shelf Life

Storytelling isn't just for Hollywood anymore. It's slowly become part of successful business cultures. Even the National Institute for Occupational Safety and Health now uses storytelling as part of its safety training. Major corporations like Intel, Nestlé, and Samsung apply storytelling techniques for innovation, planning, marketing, and product design.

Organizations are turning to new media to convey their stories in YouTube videos, the leading form of short-subject digital storytelling. Quick stories can inspire, inform, and advocate for change. They can demonstrate quantifiable enhancements and solve problems.

Stories can enhance productivity, reward performance, demonstrate values, capture lessons learned, and preserve corporate heritage to create understanding and change in organizations.

Stories Inspire and Inform

91

One of the world's richest men is not only a self-made billionaire, he's also a master storyteller. Coincidence, not a chance. Warren Buffett, CEO of Berkshire Hathaway, ditches dry facts and replaces them with aw-shucks stories.

Why does the greatest investor America has ever produced generate stories? For the same reason that you're learning how be a better conveyor—to create clarity, not confusion. Buffett purposefully chooses to help people understand what he's talking about via plain and simple stories so they'll "get it" and choose to take action. That's knowledge management.

Let's consider a story Buffett shared in a recent annual letter to shareholders to create clarity. He focused on one of Berkshire Hathaway's most profitable investments, See's Candies, whose earnings had skyrocketed from $5 million to $82 million:

> Just as Adam and Eve kick-started an activity that led to six billion humans, See's has given birth to multiple new streams of cash for us. The biblical command to "be fruitful and multiply" is one we take seriously at Berkshire.

Smart Stories Have a Longer Shelf Life Than Mind-Numbing Facts

Smart stories have a long shelf life—far longer than mind-numbing facts. They break through workplace communiclutter and stick like glue. Like a good movie, they help us to absorb, retain, and repeat information and ideas.

I can read your mind. You're thinking, "But I'm not Warren Buffett. I'm not a Hollywood producer. I'm not even a natural storyteller." That may be true. Up until today, you may have been a humdrum conveyor, pounding people with dry factoids. How do you suddenly morph into a storyteller? You start by telling the right story at the right time.

Following are a few business storytelling tips and three tactics.

Consider a classic: President Ronald Reagan's "It's Morning Again" television reelection commercial in 1984. It was a success story that captured the mood of the nation and, as a result, the majority of votes. Here's the text of the commercial:

STORIES TACTIC 1
Tell Success Stories That Feature a Positive Future

> *It's morning again in America. Today, more men and women will go to work than ever before in our country's history. With interest rates at about half the record highs of 1980, nearly two thousand families today will buy new homes, more than at any time in the past four years. This afternoon, sixty-five hundred young men and women will be married. And with inflation at less than half of what it was just four years ago, they can look forward with confidence to the future. It's morning again in America. And, under the leadership of President Reagan, our country is prouder and stronger and better. Why would we ever want to return to where we were less than four short years ago?*

You may not have thought about your organization's history as a story before, but chances are, this is your best "a-ha" narrative.

Purposefully gazing in the rear-view mirror to craft a story conveys unmistakable understanding.

(As a side note, did you notice that the "Morning in America" campaign is anchored in threes, whose power you discovered in our previous chapter? Look near the end of the commercial: "Prouder, Stronger, Better" is the ad's theme. It was also reportedly the original title of the winning campaign.)

TIPS   *Now it's your turn to craft a success story. Here are a few tips:*

What successes can you identify in your organization? (Or your personal leadership?) What did you accomplish? How are people benefiting as a result? This is your story's purpose and passion.

Success stories must have significance. Link your tale to concrete outcomes and your story will be a winner. It should ring with optimism and hope for a positive future. Share what has changed significantly for the better.

Your story should resonate. It must be truthful enough to shake skeptics and reveal a universal truth that motivates others to act. Aim to strike a chord with your audience, not merely to be an historian.

It must be distinctive. If it sounds like the same-old, same-old, your story will likely be ignored. Copycat versions leave most people feeling cheated. Your story may have a familiar element to it, but it should be distinctive enough that it compels a new understanding.

End on a positive note. Leave your listeners with a bit of feel-good stimulation. Don't ruin it by letting your story simply peter out. End with a purpose, a positive lesson.

One of the bestselling business stories of all time is *Who Moved My Cheese?* by Spencer Johnson.

This short how-to fable, a runaway bestseller released in 1998, is a corporate hit. Many employees have been required to read it, write reports about it, or break into groups and discuss it in corporate training seminars.

Managers love its message about handling change and moving forward. Some call it life changing, almost biblical. To be fair, others resent it and poke holes in it, deriding it as too simple and a waste of an hour to read a dopey modern-day Aesop's tale. Still others believe that corporations buy the book in bulk and schedule training sessions in order to prepare employees for mass layoffs.

If you haven't read the parable (either freely or unwillingly), *Who Moved My Cheese?* is about two mice, Sniffy and Scurry, and two "little people," Hem and Haw. They react differently when their food is moved to a different corner of the maze. The mice are agile and quickly move ahead to find new cheese. The humans are paralyzed by analysis until, finally, they adapt and find more cheese too. The message, of course, is that change is necessary and good.

The book has moved more than twelve million copies and continues to sell long after no-nonsense, data-driven, how-to business books by

STORIES TACTIC 2
Think Simple and Spry

legends like Jack Welch and Bill Gates have faded from the bestseller lists.

The slice of cheese I'm focusing on here involves how to convey a story to a business audience: keep it simple and spry.

TIPS   *Here are a few tips to be a simple and spry storyteller:*

Have a clear purpose. What is the specific idea that you're trying to help people understand? How will it change things? What, specifically, do you want them to learn? Keep the story's essence in mind and resist the urge to incorporate too many lessons.

Anchor it. Remember to anchor your story by starting with the basics like time and place. This will signal that it's a story. Don't skip the big picture or you'll lose people, leading to confusion, not clarity.

Trim the fat. Don't get bogged down in excess details. Your story is a means to the end, not the end itself. Share enough specifics to ignite imaginations, but not so many that your listeners get lost in irrelevant details.

Think execution. A story in a business setting must be specific enough for others to determine if they have the time, manpower, and finances to implement it. How will they put this into operation? What's the cost of not doing it? If you don't make these things clear, your audience won't get it and won't do it.

Ever been subjected to a bad storyteller? The best stories in the world can go bad if they're poorly delivered. How do you get it right? Strike a balance between sounding prepared and sounding unrehearsed. The best storytellers know their exact destination, but they stay open to detours that are in the audience's best interest.

Back to Warren Buffett. Does he sound like he's reading when he tells stories at Berkshire Hathaway's annual stockholders' meeting, or does he sound off-the-cuff? Of course, he sounds spontaneous. However, he didn't just make the story up on the spot. He planned to incorporate it, somehow, some way, and you should, too. That's what I call "planned spontaneity." You plan, but you sound spontaneous when you deliver the story.

Need tips on how to do this?

Relive it as you tell it. Adapt your story to the situation. Make it real so the audience can relate. If you're presenting to a group, step out from behind the podium and speak conversationally. Don't be stiff.

Make it about them, not you. Help your audience to envision themselves in the story. Tell it from the perspective of someone who's similar to them, not just from your own viewpoint.

Share superlatives when appropriate. A superlative is an adjective or adverb that denotes an extreme or unsurpassed level. Think *SportsCenter:* Sports programs live for smashed records and spectacular standouts. However, you can use superlatives, too. For example, let's say you're

STORIES TACTIC 3
Deliver Stories with "Planned Spontaneity"

TIPS

Portion Control: Manage Your Message so You Don't Bog Others Down

talking about three people: Sarah, Jim, and Joan. Sarah is the oldest, perhaps Jim is the strongest, and maybe Joan is the smallest of the group. People love and understand comparisons. If your group is the most profitable (or any other superlative), feature that prominently in your story and it will stick.

Try alliteration. Alliteration is one of the literary tools most commonly used to spark understanding. It's the repetition of a leading consonant sound in a phrase: for example, March Madness, The Last Lecture, and *Horton Hears a Who*. Why use it? Because it sparks accurate recall and encourages people to repeat it.

You are a storyteller. We all are. You may not have billions like Buffett or be cheesy like Spencer Johnson, but you can make people laugh, listen, and learn.

Your stories can help others process very complex information quickly and create leaps in understanding.

Convey Review and Action Plan

Use Portion Control To Manage Information

The key to conveying is portion control, which helps you manage even the most complicated messages. As a result, people can process your information more accurately and they'll grasp the exact take-aways that you desire. You talk less, but say more.

Conveying Prevents Information Overload

Successful conveying leads to rapid clarity. When you convey smartly, your listeners quickly and fully understand your points. Smart conveying skills allow you to convince your listeners to act.

STRATEGY 1
The Eyes Trump the Ears

People respond most positively to what they see rather than what they hear because vision is the dominant sense. Rather than relying on the spoken word to convey, add appropriate visuals to create clearer understanding for faster results.

What Could I Improve?

❑ TACTIC 1: SHOW CONTRAST

❑ TACTIC 2: RETHINK POWERPOINT

❑ TACTIC 3: LINK IT, MOVE IT—USE THE SOCIAL MEDIA

❑ OTHER _____

My Action Plan:

_____

_____

_____

STRATEGY 2

Talk in Triplets

Three is the world's most powerful number for receiving information. The mind craves information in multiples of three, making it a shortcut to convey successfully. Use it to save time.

What Could I Improve?

❑ TACTIC 1: PRE-LOAD THREE CHOICES

❑ TACTIC 2: THINK NARROW AND DEEP

❑ TACTIC 3: DESIRED CHOICE FIRST

❑ OTHER _____

My Action Plan:

_____

_____

_____

STRATEGY 3
Tell Stories

People are engaged when they hear a relevant story. Stories are a direct route to understanding that gives your information a longer shelf life than mind-numbing facts.

What Could I Improve?

☐ TACTIC 1: TELL SUCCESS STORIES THAT FEATURE A POSITIVE FUTURE

☐ TACTIC 2: THINK SIMPLE AND SPRY

☐ TACTIC 3: DELIVER WITH "PLANNED SPONTANEITY"

☐ OTHER _____

My Action Plan:

_____

_____

_____

My Current Approach

People get confused/misunderstand me when I . . .

_____

_____

People understand me clearly when I . . .

_____

_____

Why do I approach conveying in these ways?

_____

_____

Next Step

Once you've conveyed powerfully and managed information, you're well on your way to convincing people to commit to action, which you'll discover in the next section.

HABIT 3: CONVINCE

MANAGING ACTION

Create Commitment to Influence Decisions, Actions, Results

10 SIGNS
YOU MAY BE A WEAK CONVINCER

(And Where to Turn to Conquer Them)

1 People resist committing to your ideas, or they frequently delay making decisions concerning your ideas or requests.

ISSUE: CONVINCING ESSENTIALS

FIND HELP: page 109

2 You change your mind a lot, or strike others as being indecisive.

ISSUE: SOUND DECISIVE—STOP TAGGING AND HEDGING

FIND HELP: page 118

3 You sometimes lack confidence, causing you to withhold sharing ideas.

ISSUE: SOUND DECISIVE—CONTRIBUTE TO MEETINGS

FIND HELP: page 121

4 At times, people question your sincerity or accuse you of being a yes-man to those who are higher-up in your organization.

ISSUE: SOUND DECISIVE—VOICE YOUR OPINIONS WITH SINCERITY

FIND HELP: page 123

5 You frequently present your ideas before running them past other stakeholders to get their feedback.

ISSUE: TRANSFER OWNERSHIP—USE PEER POWER

FIND HELP: page 130

6 You rarely explain the reason why you want people to do things.

ISSUE: TRANSFER OWNERSHIP—REVEAL YOUR REASONING

FIND HELP: page 132

7 You make decisions alone, without input.

ISSUE: TRANSFER OWNERSHIP—LET IT FLOW

FIND HELP: page 133

8 You've been told that your voice sounds as if you're disinterested or angry, even when you're not.

ISSUE: ADJUST YOUR ENERGY—YOUR VOICE

FIND HELP: page 141

9 People often ask you what's wrong because they think that you look mad.

ISSUE: ADJUST YOUR ENERGY—YOUR FACE

FIND HELP: page 144

10 You have a mannerism or body language that sometimes distracts others.

Turn the Page for Help

ISSUE: ADJUST YOUR ENERGY—YOUR BODY

FIND HELP: page 147

9

Why Convince?

Action Management

Are you an influential person with enormous power? Do you get things done through others? Do you save time and money by inspiring higher performance? Are you capable of creating growth, innovation, and profitability by convincing others to act? If you answered yes to all of these questions, congratulations, you can stop reading now.

Are you brilliant at business strategy, but poor at convincing others to do what must be done? Do you find yourself frustrated while communicating because others don't easily buy into your ideas?

Influence Others to Act without Delay

Whether you relate more to the first or second paragraph or find yourself somewhere in between, the answers are crucial to your success, both in business and in your personal life. The ability to positively, and quickly, influence others is a core leadership skill that produces superior results. In addition, it's more important now than ever before, because speed to market has become critical.

Biggest Blunders Manipulating and Arm-Twisting

Influential people use their power to sway behaviors, decisions, actions, and outcomes. They revitalize organizations by inspiring individuals and departments to meet or exceed goals. They cut through clutter and make things happen.

Let's get clear about what I mean by convincing. There are two common misperceptions:

First, convincing does *not* mean manipulating or arm-twisting. The difference is intent. Manipulators focus on their own needs and theirs alone. They're determined to get their way, regardless of the impact on others. They'll steamroll, lie, or omit the truth in order to get what they want.

True, manipulators often get their way, but their success is short-lived. They earn merely compliance, not commitment. You do things for manipulators grudgingly, because you feel you have to, not because you want to.

Second, convincers don't have to be ultra-charismatic. The ability to convince others is not a genetic gift like singing ability. It can be learned. Most convincers don't captivate crowds as successfully as Apple CEO Steve Jobs, a seasoned presenter who takes the stage with the rock-star status of Mick Jagger. Most convincers are more like Microsoft founder Bill Gates, who's not exactly known for his dazzling presentation skills.

However, both men know the secret: Convincing is not a thunderbolt event. It's not an isolated, once-and-done occurrence. It's a process that unfolds incrementally—**Connect-Convey-Convince**®—to change hearts and minds and compel others to action. It's the third and final step. If you've connected and conveyed properly, convincing should be the easiest step.

Let's focus on Apple for a moment. Have you ever been to an Apple Store? They're like the new bars of the digital age. People linger for hours, sharing success stories and soaking up tips. The environment, including the Genius Bar, is buzzing with ideas and energy. When people leave the Apple Store, they're often excited to spread the word. They go forth to recruit friends and strangers to the Apple life.

Why are people so committed to Apple? For the same reason that you're committed to your own favorite brands. You're convinced that you've discovered something special and you proudly pass it on.

Create Commitment, Not Compliance

To bring this together, consider how Steve Jobs connected, conveyed, and convinced to bring his company's most successful product ever, the iPod, to life. First, he connected with consumers' wants and values. In the late 1990s, he learned from the success of Napster, the popular if illegal peer-to-peer file-sharing platform, that millions of people valued cobbling together all of their favorite songs in a digital format. Then, Jobs conveyed his vision for a groundbreaking digital device to his team of engineers so they clearly understood the functions and cool design that he envisioned. Finally, he convinced engineers to knock themselves out to get the product to market in 2001. How did Jobs convince engineers to deliver what others thought was impossible?

They bought into the idea because they wanted iPods too.

From "Over My Dead Body" to Yes!

However, that wasn't all. Jobs also convinced artists and the major record labels to grant his forthcoming iTunes Music Store the digital rights to their catalogs of songs. How did he do that? Many influential people in the music industry, like successful producer Dr. Dre, were on record as saying they would never sign away digital rights to their music. "Over my dead body" was the sentiment.

Steve Jobs changed minds and convinced heavy hitters to get on board with the iTunes Music Store. How did he pull that off? The music industry was suffering from piracy issues. Jobs understood the issue of protecting intellectual property. He led them to discover and envision success in a new, aboveboard format that would forever change how music was sold and benefit them financially.

If you're serious about gaining agreement and getting things done through others, you should layer the convincing skill onto what you learned in the previous sections about connecting and conveying. You'll discover how-to tips in the following three chapters.

You'll learn to convince by sounding decisive, even if you don't feel that way. You'll discover how to prevent sounding wishy-washy, which convinces people that you merely want validation, not action. You'll learn why it's important to contribute to meetings, and how to stop qualifying and hedging.

You'll also discover how to convince by transferring ownership of your ideas to others. You'll learn to gain strength by involving your peers. You'll learn how to purposefully explain how you got from point A to point B in order to get people off the fence. You'll also see how managing inaccuracies and being transparent earns people's trust.

You'll see how "adjusting your energy" may be just the boost you need to convince people to act. Did you know that using the right muscles could make you appear interested and approachable? On the other hand, that failing to use them leads others to conclude that you just don't care. Alternatively, how about your voice? Do you know the most convincing tone of voice to move people into your corner?

Finally, you'll discover how the principle of reciprocity may be holding you back from getting what you want. You'll learn to speak with the passion of someone who's totally committed in order to earn the reciprocity of others' commitment.

What's Holding You Back?

Today's modern communication tools—caller ID, text, e-mail, and such—make it easier than ever for people to dodge and deflect your attempts to convince them to do something. It's a tremendous challenge to influence behaviors, decisions, actions, and outcomes in our fast-paced, electronically focused world.

Convince in a smart manner, and you'll improve your ability to sell ideas, products, services, or even yourself. You'll experience a dramatic increase in your ability to get things done through others.

Read on for techniques on how to start convincing others to act.

10

Sound Decisive
Stop Babbling and Backpedaling

When you open your mouth to speak, do your words sound decisive or wishy-washy? Do you display confidence or come across as insecure? Do people take you seriously or ignore what you say?

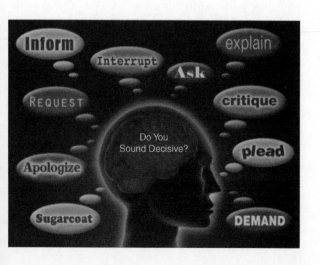

Sound Like a Wimp and You'll Be Treated Like One

If it's the latter, it's time to stop wavering and start firming up your communications. If you sound like a wimp, you'll be treated like one.

The language of leadership is decisive. Using weak language strips you of power and blocks your ability to convince others and determine outcomes. Your capacity to communicate decisions is one of the most telling measures of your power and influence. Gridlock and delay are the outcomes of indecision. When you sound indecisive, you're collapsing under your own weight. You're inadvertently sabotaging your ability to persuade others to make things happen.

When you sound decisive, you capitalize on opportunities and conquer obstacles. Making good decisions quickly and speaking with confidence is a hallmark of a high-performance leader. Confidence is contagious. If you sound self-assured, people will respond with confidence to you and your contributions.

Has this ever happened to you? You shared an idea that was ignored, only to hear it later heralded as a great idea when someone else said it. Chances are the problem was a lack of conviction in how you said it. You may have used weak, wimpy language and come across as indecisive. The copycat took ownership by saying it more conclusively. That's why he got the credit.

If you want to get credit for your ideas, there's a simple fix: sound more decisive. Otherwise, you run the risk of being invisible while others grab the limelight.

Coming across as indecisive is more prevalent in women than men, but it's not gender-specific. Many people damage their credibility by wavering and sounding uncertain. Are you a vacillator? Here are a few telltale signs:

Habitual Back-Pedaling Damages Credibility

- Need others' approval before committing
- Refuse to take a stand
- Look to others for validation
- Sound unsure of yourself
- Use hesitant words
- Habitually avoid conflict and criticism
- Appease or pacify to avoid confrontation
- Are overly apologetic
- Quickly back down when challenged

Confidence is the key to sounding decisive. In order to convince others, you must first sound as if you've convinced yourself. When you sound decisive, you'll:

- Be better understood
- Gain clout and respect
- Get credit for your ideas
- Run more effective meetings
- Stop wasting time by waffling
- Say "no" more powerfully
- Get to "yes" more quickly
- Transform from weak to powerful

Sounding decisive and convincing people to act is situational, like all communication.

Stop Tagging and Hedging

Following are three tactics and many tips to help you sound more decisive to trigger action.

Tagging means turning a perfectly good declarative sentence into a question by adding a short question at the end. It turns a statement into a request for validation. Hedging means starting a sentence with weak words in order to dodge commitment.

These two habits imply that you're unsure of your facts, the situation, or yourself. They're poison to the process of persuasion because they signal neediness, uncertainty, or a lack of confidence. When you tag and hedge, at best, people don't commit; at worst, aggressive people take the opportunity to pounce.

Tagging.   Jane is a habitual tagger. Let's look at one hour in her workday. In a conversation with her boss, she says, "This is a good plan . . . don't you think?" as she seeks to validate her opinion. To a project member she says, "We should call off the meeting and take the afternoon to get things done . . . don't you think?" again weakening her stand by asking for validation. To her cubicle mate who always talks incredibly loud on the phone, she says feebly, "It's a little hard to concentrate . . . okay?"

Tagging means adding on phrases such as:

" . . . isn't that right?"

" . . . don't you think?"

" . . . okay?"

" . . . all right?"

A tag is a small addition to a sentence, but its consequences are huge. It gives away your power by signaling that you need validation or approval before you'll commit to making a decision.

Why should others commit if you won't?

Some people even tag their names by vocal lifting, which means lifting the inflection at the end of the sentence: "My name is Connie? I'm an executive communication coach?"

This is not to say that tagging isn't useful on occasion, such as when you aim to gain agreement. Some weak expressions can be powerful in the right settings, and vice versa. The difference between good taggers and damaging taggers is intent. Powerful people tag purposefully and sparingly. They use the occasional tag decisively to win consensus and gain agreement. Weak communicators use tags to gain validation.

Habitual Tagging Sounds Wishy-Washy

Hedging. Here are a few examples of hedging your way into a sentence:

"I'm not an expert, but . . . "

"I could be wrong, but . . . "

"I guess what I'm saying is . . . "

"I kind of feel like . . . "

"I'm only an assistant, but . . . "

"I'm probably the only person who feels this way, but . . . "

Habitual hedging makes you sound like you doubt your own words. You're hiding behind words and giving yourself a trapdoor to dodge personal commitment. Beating around the bush adds no value to a sentence and undermines your authority. Simply put, hedging sounds wishy-washy and weak.

Hedgers often avoid challenging other people's ideas. They can't stand opposition. It's absolutely damaging because others conclude that they have weak ideas and lack backbone.

Smart hedges. Smart hedging is a different story. It's purposeful. In these cases, hedging is not only appropriate, it's wise. The trick is to soften by choosing smart hedging words like these:

- might
- may
- consider
- appears to
- could
- should
- seems to

The next time you catch yourself sounding uncertain by tagging or hedging, ask yourself: Is it purposeful in order to convince others to act, or is it from a lack of confidence? If it's the latter, don't do it.

It's crucial to contribute to meetings if you want to convince others to see your viewpoints and act on them.

Do you have a habit of staying quiet during meetings? Did you know that prolonged silence—the kind that's born from a lack of confidence—damages your credibility?

That's what happened to Don. He was good at communicating in most situations, but not with superiors. He turned to jelly around executives.

Don is a director at the corporate headquarters of a global consumer products company. After ten years in the position, he felt he deserved a promotion to vice president. However, Don wasn't perceived as VP material. Why, because whenever he got the opportunity to attend executive meetings, he stayed as quiet as a church mouse.

Don's boss wondered why he didn't contribute. He thought there were two possibilities: (1) Don didn't have anything to contribute, or (2) Don didn't know *how* to contribute. The difference was critical. If it were the former, Don would not be promoted: if the latter, the problem could be solved and Don could advance.

Turns out, Don stifled himself because he was afraid of saying something stupid in front of higher-ups. In other words, he lacked executive presence in the presence of executives.

Once he overcame this fear by using the techniques you're about to read, he started contributing and was promoted to vice president.

Ann experienced the same thing when she joined a nonprofit organization's board of directors. She was the first and only female board member in its fifty-year history. For the first two meetings, Ann settled into her seat at the table and stayed quiet. Following her second silent meeting, Jack, the board president, called her. "Ann, what's with you? Why aren't you adding anything? I brought you on the board because I thought you'd be a strong contributor," said Jack. Ann replied, "Well, Jack, I wanted to take some time to size up the players and see how the board really worked." "Time's up," said Jack. "If you don't make contributions at the table soon, you'll be labeled as indecisive and treated like a lightweight."

Ann discovered that judgments about your leadership abilities are inferred from the way you contribute. She learned that people size you up to decide if your ideas merit their support and commitment to action.

TIPS   *Here are a few tips:*

Use planned spontaneity.   If you're anxious or uncertain in new surroundings, prepare in advance to contribute something on a specific topic. Review the agenda before the meeting and search for a topic where you can add value. Done properly, planned spontaneity is stealth. It sounds like you just thought it up on the spot and earns others' respect.

Be direct.   Don't sound ambiguous when making requests or telling subordinates what to do. Spell it out directly. Indirectness leads others to

conclude that your requests and directives are unimportant and can be overlooked.

Invite opposing viewpoints. Those who avoid opposition risk coming across as insecure or arrogant. Ask others to voice their concerns.

Don't be invisible. Trust your gut, stop second-guessing yourself, and get in the game. Contribute with an assertive voice, not a passive one.

Get a mentor. Seek out a role model who's earned other people's respect by being a decisive communicator. Ask that person to critique you and help you appear more confident and influential.

DECISIVE TACTIC 3
Voice Your Opinions With Sincerity

Whether you agree or disagree with someone, it's important to sound decisive and sincere when voicing an opinion. Don't be a yes-man who merely agrees in order to get positive face time. In addition, don't be malleable, which is often an attempt to be perceived as easy to get along with. Neither of these tactics comes from the heart, and they're both revealed as insincere over time. Be honest when sharing your opinions.

Which brings us to a form of communication that is often botched by a lack of sincerity: apologizing. Apologizing in a smart fashion can bolster your credibility and convince others to change their minds and take positive action.

Don't toss around "I'm sorry" like a football on Thanksgiving Day. Some people over-apologize, dripping with contrition, which damages their credibility. Others rush to retract merely to protect their backsides, which is perceived as insincere. Both of these tactics are ineffective. Like antibiotics, apologies become ineffective with overuse or misuse.

The trick is to understand the art of the apology and follow the right steps.

TIPS   *Here are some tips to generate goodwill with a contrite but classy apology:*

Don't sidestep. If an issue embarrasses you, you might instinctively avoid it in an effort to save face. Instead, you'll look insensitive. A good, honest apology mends relationships and reputations. When you apologize, you convince others that you're confident and empathetic.

Hit the hot button. Focus specifically on the emotional hot button. If you're criticized for being irresponsible, for example, apologize for your lack of judgment.

State the solution. If there's a remedy to your transgression, share exactly how you're going to make it right. This will prevent future arrows from being slung at you.

Focus on the recipient. An apology involves much more than a quick "Oops—sorry!" Make sure the recipient knows that you fully understand the impact of your transgression and that you won't let it happen again.

Don't blame the victim. You'll sound pompous and insincere. Don't begin with "If I offended anybody . . . " That sounds like you're blaming a resentful person for being overly sensitive to remarks that you obviously didn't intend as an affront. Instead, take responsibility. Say something like, "I offended you and I'm sorry."

Time is of the essence. Apologize as soon as possible. In today's Internet age, you can't wait for the Web to spread bad things before you express your contrition, or people will be convinced that you're guilty and don't care.

Don't apologize repeatedly for a single mistake. Don't dwell on the mistake or constantly remind others of it. Focus your energies on correcting the error. If you spend too much time peering in the rear-view mirror, you're bound to crash into something head-on.

Don't inflict wounds. Lines like "No offense, but . . . " and "Don't take this personally, but . . . " are passive-aggressive. You're saying one thing, but you mean the opposite. What you're about to say is personal, and yes, it's likely to offend. So instead of qualifying it, be honest and get to the point kindly but decisively.

It's time to sound decisive. Don't babble and backpedal. The bottom line is this: Communicate with confidence and you'll convince people to buy in and act.

11

Transfer Ownership
Create Commitment, Not Compliance

Transferring ownership means shifting your ideas and decisions to others so they will embrace them and act on them. It has enormous consequences for both personal and organizational buy-in. It's the difference between others feeling actively involved in their destiny and, therefore, committed to it versus feeling forced to comply. Buy-in leads people to change behaviors, decisions, and actions.

This is how leading sales executives build wealth. It's also how great leaders enable people in their organizations to meet goals and overcome power struggles. Lee Iacocca, who revived Chrysler as its CEO and president in the 1980s, was a transfer master. He inspired others by asking them to share in both the obligations and the successes of the car company. Iacocca set the right tone to convince others to buy in. In his book, *Where Have All the*

People Should Feel as if They're Volunteering, Not Surrendering.

Leaders Gone, he recalled using words such as these to transfer ownership and make things happen:

> *We have a tough task ahead of us. The challenges are formidable. But together we can do it. It'll take everyone—the employees, the dealers, the suppliers, the union, the government—and we're asking for your help.*

A good leader wants people to own what they do and take responsibility for their actions. Transferring ownership helps build morale, retention, productivity, and sales. It also encourages commitment to you as the leader. Your leadership can be rendered powerless by others' individual or collective decisions to ignore or overturn you. You can force people to comply with your requests or demands temporarily, but people will make their own decisions about commitment, which they can hide or share with others to transfer ownership.

Let Them Own It and They'll Do It

Let's start with this premise: Self-discovery is the most persuasive argument. It's powerful when people feel they've arrived at a decision by themselves. Therefore, if you transfer your ideas and decisions to others so they can take ownership, you're more likely to get positive results.

Let's look to Nike, led by CEO Phil Knight, as a living example of this principle. Do Nike advertisements instruct you to buy their products? No. They show you athletic superstars who've capitalized on their potential while wearing Nike products. They let you arrive at the decision to buy Nike products yourself. You're convinced that Nike products will help your performance, too.

The Ritz-Carlton hospitality organization has also mastered transferring ownership. Every day, employees gather to discuss one of the company's core values, including their credo, "We are ladies and gentlemen serving ladies and gentlemen." This transferring of ownership ensures that the organization's values of warmth and genuine caring are shifted successfully from leadership to frontline employees. The legendary Ritz-Carlton gold standard of hospitality was built in part by transferring ownership, and has led to strong relationships and memorable experiences with both employees and guests.

Do You Empower or Impede?

Another example of transferring ownership in action is your friendly in-home party selling kitchen gear, makeup, candles, or even sex toys. Multilevel home party companies, led by Tupperware, have built business models on transferring ownership from their companies to party hosts who, in turn, transfer it to their friends by sending invitations to attend a "party." Why do you buy at these in-home selling shows? You feel obligated. You come for wine and cheese; you leave after shelling out 20 bucks for a doohickey. In-home selling companies use the social network—and sometimes, guilt trips—to influence purchases.

You don't have to lead an organization, host a party, own a hotel, or sell products in order to use this technique. Anyone can reach out and empower others to adopt ideas as their own and take action.

Following are three tactics to transfer ownership:

Use Peer Power

We can all take a lesson from the skilled, if shameless, TV infomercial marketers. They've made billions by transferring ownership of their products to our hearts and minds. Lest you think I've lost *my* mind, let's get one thing straight: I'm not advocating that you reduce yourself to the infomercials' brazen exaggerations and pure hokum. Quite the contrary. I'm suggesting that you learn the skill of transferring ownership through peer power.

In their quest to move turbo cookers, thigh reducers, colon cleansers, and mineral makeup, infomercial marketers hit pay dirt with their average man-on-the-street testimonials. Advertisers are keenly aware of the selling power of testimonials from ordinary people who choose the product, use it, and love to tell others about it. They speak glowingly about how the product has changed their lives, and in the process they transfer their goodwill to you. (Of course, not all of these testimonials are aboveboard. The technique has been so successful that counterfeit convincers have crept in. Paid actors now deliver some testimonials.) People are persuaded by the actions of others.

TIPS

Here's how to use peer power in the workplace:

Seek commitment from key influencers. Seek out the people and stakeholders in your workplace who routinely influence other people, either positively or negatively. Secure their commitment before meetings where you'll introduce your ideas. Their commitment will fill your pipeline with others.

Tap into trustworthy, popular people. Oprah Winfrey transferred her peer power to Barack Obama in the early stages of his presidential campaign. She prompted many of her followers to pour into Obama's rallies, which translated into votes. Why? Because Oprah's followers trusted her. You can do this, too, by asking a popular, trustworthy person to help rally the troops to your cause.

Use an alternating format. In her daily TV program, Oprah shifts between talking to her guests and speaking directly to the audience. You can do this in meetings by addressing everyone as a group and then keying in on powerful people who will back you up and lend you their support.

Get them to take a stand. When people publicly proclaim their position, they are most likely to stay true to their decision. Have you ever served on a jury? Those who use a visible show of hands to vote are the most hardened toward their positions. Use this principle by encouraging supportive people to commit out loud to solidify commitments.

Salt the tip jar. Take a lesson from smart bartenders who salt the tip jar with dollar bills. Why? They know it implies that others are tipping and that you should, too. Learn from this by requesting written testimonials to help spread the word that you or your ideas have the backing of others. Testimonials increase the odds that others will follow suit.

Convince yourself first. If you're not fully bought in, smart people will know it and act accordingly.

Reveal Your Reasoning

Rudy Giuliani, the mayor of New York City during the tragic events of September 11, 2001, was a master of this. He got front and center after the terrorist attack, keeping citizens informed of his decisions and sharing the reasons behind them as he led the city in the wake of the attacks.

Why is this critical? When they don't hear the real reason behind a decision, many people will assign it the worst possible reasoning. It's human nature. Office gossips assume the worst and spread their poison, leading to grudges, resistance, and poor execution.

When I ask leaders for their secret weapons to convince resistant people to act, most say they simply back up and explain why they want people to do things in the first place. That's how they enlist an army to become part of the solution. It's easier to support something when you understand what you're trying to solve and why.

TIPS   *Here are a few pointers to reveal your reasoning:*

Get out front with it quickly. Don't let people draw their own conclusions. Don't allow uninformed or ill-informed people to convince others that your idea or decision is not in their best interest.

Define, don't defend. If you're explaining a challenging situation, focus on what you're doing to overcome it rather than allowing yourself to dissect it. Don't put blood in the water or the sharks will tear you apart.

Put it in writing. Decisions become real when they're committed to paper. Let people see it so they believe it. Nothing is truly settled until it's committed to writing.

Get them to write it down, too. A power shift occurs when people physically write down their commitments. It becomes real and they live up to it. The very act of writing something creates commitment.

What if you don't really approve? Let's be honest. Most jobs involve supporting the occasional idea or initiative that you don't personally approve of. Find something to like about it that doesn't compromise your fundamental beliefs or values and then explain that part as honestly as possible.

Let them volunteer, not surrender. Don't push and shove. Be patient and let people reach their own conclusions.

Ownership can now be transferred in both directions, because the Internet changed everything. Pre-Internet, company leaders rallied the troops through reports and annual speeches. Now, in our interactive world, everyone seeks audiences and input. A team in Asia Pacific can advocate for change at company headquarters in Akron, Ohio. A project group can bypass their team lead and call for her ouster online.

Whether you're trying to convince one or one thousand, here are ways to let it flow to transfer ownership:

TRANSFER
TACTIC 3
Let It Flow

TIPS

Reach out and encourage others to speak up. Break the barrier. Set up a chat room where people can ask questions and provide feedback. If you don't start one, others will. Better to be involved rather than blindsided. If you're not part of the conversation, people will speak on your behalf, and you may not agree with what they say. It's best to participate in order to cultivate.

Respond to that feedback. Here's the deal: Once people speak up, they expect to hear from you. Don't ignore it. Acknowledge everything and move on the input that's actionable.

Monitor Web entries. How do you know that others are transferring ideas on the Web about topics that involve you? Google Alerts offers free e-mail updates on Web entries. Let Google track the Web and keep you updated when others post new information. You'll learn about dissatisfaction and pleasure by monitoring blogs, chat rooms, and Web entries.

Use smart Q&A. In meetings, always end on a positive question from a peer. Tie your answer back to your key point to capitalize on commitments.

Reinforce urgency. We're all rushed and have too much work on our plates, so we focus on deadlines. Impose a time limit to create urgency. You'll move from the backburner to the front burner to keep the commitment flowing.

Use thoughtful gestures. Charities use this technique. Have you ever gotten a pack of personalized return address labels in the mail along with a request for a donation? When mailings include small, unsolicited gifts, their success rates nearly double. The unspoken rule is that receivers are beholden to repay the kindness. Thoughtfulness has its rewards, so try thoughtful gestures.

Don't underestimate the power of transferring ownership, or you'll underperform. Let others feel personally involved by transferring ownership of your ideas and decisions to them, and you'll increase your capabilities to convince them to act.

12

Adjust Your Energy
Start Attracting, Stop Repelling

Don't you enjoy being around energetic, positive people? People who are stimulating and make you feel good gain your commitment faster and easier.

Most of us could use an energy boost. I don't mean morphing into Jim Cramer from *Mad Money,* gesturing wildly, sharing rapid-fire opinions, and yelling his catchphrase, "Booya!"—that works for Cramer, but it would likely be career suicide in your workplace. What I mean by "adjusting your energy" is combining your purpose with the right level of passion. Sometimes you need to ramp it up; sometimes you need to tone it down. It's situational, but achieving the right energy level convinces people to act.

As you know, when you communicate with someone, it's not just the words you choose that send a message. People monitor the signals you send. Your intensity, facial expression, pitch, tone,

People Monitor You for Signals

volume, eye contact, and body language all combine to influence others. The question is, "How does your energy level come across to others?" Do others define you as energetic, stiff, disinterested, lazy, angry, determined, icy?

The signals you send are crucial for this reason: reciprocity. People give back to you what you give to them. Energy feeds on itself. Energized people create energy in others. If you look and sound engaged and self-assured, people will respond more positively to you. If you look or sound off-putting, you'll induce negative responses.

Energy Boosts Likeability

Energy boosts likability, which is a key ingredient to generate commitment from others. Likability becomes the framework for the rest of the information people gather about you and your ideas, so make it positive and upbeat.

Consider CEO Anne Mulcahy's stunning turn-around at Xerox. Mulcahy restored profitability and brought the company back from $10 billion in debt after taking over the top job in 2001. Her team responded to her positive leadership and started innovating. Stock tripled. How did she do it? She got bottom-line results from top-line smarts. Mulcahy radiates positive energy. She is a genuine, approachable leader who hits the energy sweet spot: She balances *credibility* and *likability*.

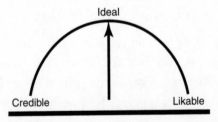

Ideal

Credible   Likable

Where do you fall on this scale? Are you perceived as tilted to the left or right? If you aim for dead center to balance your credibility and likability, you'll attract people with the right energy level for each situation and they'll be willing to go the extra mile for you.

Mulcahy's leadership underscores the effectiveness of how an energetic, authentic person can drive sustainable results. You can do this, too. Amplify your communication with the right energy. Words are never sufficient by themselves. Don't undermine your words with inconsistencies in tone. Be an authentic, congruent leader.

I saw the power of congruency up close in my years in broadcast television. The best guests were those who were consistent, matching their tone with their words: The chefs who were lively and entertaining, the CEOs who appeared thoughtful and concerned when announcing cutbacks, the authors who sounded well read. The guests who were ineffective were the types who muttered, "Glad to be here," while scowling. You get the picture.

In the studios, I learned that top communicators came across the same whether on camera or off. They didn't change their style—they just ramped up their energy levels in high-profile communications. Guests like President Bill Clinton, sex authority Dr. Ruth, and exercise guru Richard Simmons were the masters.

Then there were the TV guests whom I called "red-lighters." I won't name names, but these

Are You a "Red-Lighter?"

people were two-faced. They were chilly in person, but lit up and played energetic and nice when the camera's red tally light glowed to indicate that we were live or taping. Our crews were secretly delighted when red-lighters occasionally got caught being their true selves and were exposed as frauds. I bet you know someone like that in the business world. Are there people in your organization who kiss up to those above them on the organizational chart, but are nasty and dismissive to peers and direct reports? Don't you love it when their deception is revealed to executives?

This is all tied to energy level, because you can't fake it and sustain it. You have to feel authentic energy in order for it to be sustainable and reciprocated. How do you do this? Reconnect with your commitment. The key to your energy is to find out what drives you. What's your personal stake in what you're saying? Why do you care about it? How can it change people's lives? That's how you uncover your purpose and combine it with the right level of passion.

Influence People to Get Up and Take an Action Step

If you give presentations, your energy level is doubly important. Most presentations are dreadful. On an energy scale of one to ten, most presenters score about a two. They're boring and lack enthusiasm. Remember, presentations are opportunities to effect change. You need to motivate people to get up and take an action step. For that, you need energy. Combine purpose and passion and you'll hit your energy sweet spot.

Even if you don't do formal presentations, you need energy for phone calls, conference calls, staff meetings, webcasts, and other new media.

Your energy can be broken down into three components: voice, face, and body.

Sometimes the difference between winning and losing comes down to how people perceive your voice. I've recorded commercials and corporate videos for hundreds of clients. I don't tell you this to brag, quite the contrary. Even with years of voiceover experience, I still have to adjust my vocal energy every day.

Before heading to a studio for a recording session, I test my energy level by reading the script into a voice recorder and then playing it back. Every time I'm surprised by how incredibly boring I sound. I have to adjust my energy to more accurately project the enthusiasm I feel—and so do you.

Why does this happen? You have a skewed perception of how you sound. Your head acts like an echo chamber. Your bones reverberate when you talk, so your voice sounds bigger, more energetic, and warmer inside your head than it does when it mixes with oxygen and is transmitted to others.

Ever listened to your outgoing voice mail message or heard yourself on a voice recorder? It's shocking, isn't it? Most of us think the recording is distorted and doesn't sound like us. We're dead wrong. Digital doesn't lie. It's far more accurate than the voice you hear inside your head. What this means is that you need to kick it up a notch

ENERGY TACTIC 1
Your Voice

You Have a Skewed Perception of How You Sound

and add more energy in order to come across with warmth.

I'm not asking you to channel your inner Richard Simmons. Instead, think of your voice as an elevator. Your everyday vocal level is the ground floor. When you want to convince others, you'll need to ride the elevator to at least the second floor. Practice this by recording a few minutes of a presentation or other material as you would normally deliver it. Then play it back. Ask yourself, "Would that voice convince you to act, or would it bore you silly?" If it's the latter, adjust your energy. Try it again. This time, add more energy, smile, use gestures, use more vocal variety. When you listen to the playback, your voice will be far more engaging.

TIPS *Here's how to sound like you mean business with a warm, friendly style:*

Use vocal variety. Sameness is the death of any speaker. Don't hypnotize or lull people to sleep by speaking in the same continuous tone. Switch it up. Use all the range in your voice—the depth, the midtones, and, occasionally, the high range.

Shift the speed. Speed is another energy indicator. Slow down when you want to emphasize a point; speed up when a lively pace is appropriate. Just don't drone on at the same pace. A constant rhythm is a sedative to the ears.

Use shorter sentences. Some people sound boring because every sentence they speak is so long. Toss short sentences in as often as you can.

You'll be amazed at how this breaks monotony and makes people sit up and take notice.

Emphasize action verbs. Not every word should have the same emphasis. Use colorful verbs. Underscore them. Hit on the action. Don't be humdrum.

Try the power pause. After you make an important point, let it breathe. Don't rush to fill the silence. People are intrigued by momentary silence, so throw in a pause when you need to command attention and gain power. The power pause signals that what you just said (or are about to say) is important and the listener should let it sink in.

Thin is not in. Trying to look skinny by sucking in your stomach thins out your voice. Your voice is shaped by your breath support. Breathing too shallowly and speaking from the throat creates a thinner, weaker voice. Instead, breathe deeply from the diaphragm by pushing out your gut. This simple act can make your voice sound a full register lower.

Don't sound kittenish. Do you want a fuller, richer, more resonant voice? That's another benefit of breathing from your diaphragm instead of your throat. Deep belly breathing removes the excess air in your voice, so you don't sound so breathy, high-pitched, and little girlish.

Check the intensity. Sometimes you need to tone it down and not come on too strong—especially when you're delivering bad or unwelcome news. At other times, you need more intensity, such as in a presentation when you're trying to inspire. Intensity trumps volume. Match your energy to the specific situation.

ENERGY TACTIC 2
Your Face

People form opinions about you with a quick glance at your face. They eyeball your mug, interpret its meaning, and respond accordingly.

Some of the most successful leaders share warm facial expressions. CEOs Phil Knight of Nike and Richard Branson of Virgin brands are approachable leaders—it's written all over their faces. Their smiles are not plastered on or manufactured, they're genuine. The same is true with Warren Buffett and Bill Gates. They appear open, agreeable, and positive, and have benefited from it.

Finance expert Suze Orman's energy comes through the TV. Her purpose and passion convince others to come along for the ride. Chances are your favorite TV personality uses an energy level that appeals to you.

Is your face dead or alive? Consider Bill Clinton and Bob Dole. See the photo of the two men at the same moment in time on CNN.

Photo credit: CNN

The constant twinkle in Bill Clinton's eyes gives the impression that he's engaged and interested. Bob Dole's lack of energy leaves the unintended impression that he's smelled something bad.

Often, we send the wrong signals unintentionally. Facial symmetry can throw us off. Dick Cheney's lopsided smile makes him look half-pleased, half-bored, even when he's smiling.

How do you show energy with your face? Easy: **TIPS**

Start looking like you care. Did you know you have more than eighty muscles stretched in layers over your cranium? Your facial expressions come from their changeable positions, and you may be sending the wrong signal based on the placement of a few muscles. A broadcaster's secret is to pull the cheek muscles up to create the impression of engagement. That's what former president Bill Clinton is doing in the picture above (and what Bob Dole is not doing). You don't have to bare your teeth in a full-blown smile to appear engaged, simply pull up the cheek muscles and you'll look interested. A nice side effect is that it also puts a twinkle in your eyes. This simple move has a profound effect on how you come across to others.

The eyes have it. You know you're supposed to establish eye contact, but do you know why? It provides feedback without words. It builds rapport because it shows patience and encouragement. Additionally, it shows respect. It's also how you look for turn-taking cues to know when to enter a conversation.

Use the opposite eye technique. The best eye contact is consistent but not constant. If anyone has ever stared you down, you know how uncomfortable that is. How do you maintain consistency? Here's another broadcaster's secret: Look at just one eye. After a while, shift to the other eye. The other person will never know what you're doing, but it creates a comfortable, steady gaze. This allows you to maintain consistent contact without staring and creeping people out.

Don't be flirty. Avoid tilting your head, which is a signal of submission. It looks coy and cute. That's not a powerful move in the workplace, unless you happen to work on the Las Vegas strip. Otherwise, keep your head on straight.

Don't look snooty. Another common mistake is to lift your chin too high. This gives the impression that you're condescending, even if it's unintentional. Habitually lifting your chin too high also creates a lot of tension in your neck, which can lead you to raise your shoulders as well. High chins and raised shoulders are generally outward signs that you're stressed out.

The truth about your smile. You've heard many times that you should smile. The truth is, it has to be a genuine smile, or it can backfire on you. Plastered on smiles don't cut it; neither do contempt smiles. Genuine smiles have a powerful effect on others because they increase your likeability. People will cut you slack if your smile appears to be heartfelt.

You've heard that body language is important, and it is. Body-talk sends messages that people decode. They size you up in seconds and draw private conclusions about whether you're credible, likable, or trustworthy.

When we see body language that we interpret as powerful and positive, we're more apt to respond positively to what we hear. Do you carry yourself like a leader who convinces others to follow you?

The key is to avoid distracting mannerisms. There's a difference between *gestures* and *mannerisms*. Mannerisms are the things you do that you're unaware of when you do them. Nervous tics like fiddling with cuffs, smoothing hair, playing with pens, and bouncing legs are all examples of distracting mannerisms.

When participants in my executive presence and presentation skills programs request to be videotaped, one of the first things we do when we play back the tapes is turn off the sound. We focus first on the body, because, as you'll remember from an earlier chapter, the eyes trump the ears. This is how we pick up any distracting mannerisms and help to eliminate them quickly.

Here are a few body talk tips:

Make it real. Gestures are most effective when they're a natural extension of the feelings you're trying to express. Gestures can reinforce your

ENERGY TACTIC 3
Your Body

TIPS

message, or they can undercut it if they come across as forced or fake. As long as your gestures match your intensity, they'll work to your advantage.

Don't stifle positive gestures. Some people mistakenly believe they talk with their hands too much. That's rare. If your arm movements distract from your words, then yes, they can be too much. However, most heartfelt gestures are consistent with your words, and therefore, they help to improve your energy level and your voice.

Quiet your lower body. Here's where most people need to tone it down. Pacing back and forth or bouncing your legs or feet is very distracting. Keep the lower body relatively quiet.

Use the power stance. When standing, keep your feet about shoulder-width apart. Soften the knees a tad. This is the best position for the lower body to come across as relaxed but powerful. It also keeps tension at a minimum.

Sit on a hip. When standing as I've described above, shift your weight from one hip to the other in order to switch it up a bit. This casual movement prevents you from pacing.

Use stress to your advantage. If you get butterflies when speaking to a group, congratulations—you're normal. I'd be more worried about you if you didn't get nervous. The difference between high performers and others is that they know how to use that stress to improve their performance. Butterflies cause your heart to race and your pulse to quicken. Use that energy, don't be afraid of it. Just take deeper breaths. Deep cleansing breaths aren't limited to Lamaze class. They help all of us keep focused and give our best effort. Shallow breathing causes more tension because your body isn't getting enough oxygen.

Conquer your mannerisms. Ask someone you trust to tell you about your habitual mannerisms so you can eliminate them.

Get a grip. Your handshake communicates your confidence, openness, and friendliness. Put it there—but not too hard, and not too soft, either. A firm handshake helps make a good first impression.

Let's finish this chapter with a final tip on how to handle stress so it doesn't sap your energy. Discover what situations create anxiety for you and learn to manage your behavior so you don't send unproductive signals. This is key to your leadership because direct reports often mimic your behavior, so you're giving them license to follow suit.

Use your passion as a positive way to boost commitment. You'll discover that it's a game-changer and can give you an edge.

Convince Review and Action Plan
Earn Commitment to Manage Action

Convincing Prevents Delays and Inactivity

The third and final habit, convincing, is the ability to influence behaviors, decisions, and successful outcomes. You'll earn commitment and inspire others to take rapid action. All while talking less.

When you convince in an influential manner, you'll consistently sell ideas, products, services, and even yourself. You'll also experience a dramatic increase in your ability to get things done with and through others.

STRATEGY 1
Sound Decisive

The language of leadership is decisive. Your capacity to confidently communicate decisions is one of the most telling measures of your power and influence. Confidence is contagious. If you sound self-assured, people will respond with confidence in your leadership and to your contributions.

What Could I Improve?

❑ TACTIC 1: STOP TAGGING AND HEDGING
❑ TACTIC 2: CONTRIBUTE TO MEETINGS
❑ TACTIC 3: VOICE YOUR OPINIONS WITH SINCERITY
❑ OTHER _____

My Notes:

_____

_____

_____

STRATEGY 2

Transfer Ownership

Shift your ideas and decisions to others so they will embrace and act on them. Good leaders want people to own what they do and take responsibility. When you transfer your ideas and decisions to others so they can take ownership, you're more likely to get positive results.

What Could I Improve?

❑ TACTIC 1: USE PEER POWER
❑ TACTIC 2: REVEAL YOUR REASONING
❑ TACTIC 3: LET IT FLOW
❑ OTHER _____

My Notes:

_____

_____

_____

STRATEGY 3

Adjust Your Energy

How does your energy level come across to others? Positive and upbeat energy boosts like-ability, which is a key ingredient to generate commitment from others. Negative energy can inadvertently cause you to come across as disinterested, angry or otherwise having a bad attitude. Adding warmth is key.

What Could I Improve?

❑ TACTIC 1: ADD WARMTH TO YOUR VOICE

❑ TACTIC 2: ADD ENERGY TO YOUR FACE

❑ TACTIC 3: POWERFUL BODY LANGUAGE

❑ OTHER _____

My Action Plan:

_____

_____

_____

My Current Approach

_____

_____

People commit and act promptly when I . . .

_____

_____

People delay or reject my ideas when I . . .

_____

_____

Why do I approach convincing in these ways?

_____

_____

Putting It All Together
Connect-Convey-Convince®

Are you convinced that it's time to talk less and say more in today's world of short attention spans? Now that you've read the book, you know that your performance and personal ratings can soar by taking three simple, yet profound, incremental steps.

3 Simple but Profound Habits:

1. *Connect* to what others want and value to grab their attention.

2. *Convey* with portion control to create clarity, not confusion.

3. *Convince* them to personally commit and take a specific action.

Capitalize on these steps and you'll have the communication horsepower to become a stellar leader. Why? These steps correspond to the three biggest communication challenges facing leaders today:

1. Getting people's attention in a distraction-driven world.

2. Cutting through information overload so others are crystal-clear on what you want or what you offer.

3. Moving people to commit to action when they're being pulled in so many other directions.

In today's communiclutter society, you cannot be a strong leader with weak communication skills. Leadership requires that you rise above the clutter to become the voice that others listen for and respond to positively.

Unfortunately, smart communication is not a skill that most people pick up in business school. I believe that's a shame, because this gives you the edge to lead at your best and outperform competitors. Chances are you've risen as far as you have already by developing strong skills in one or two of the categories. That's great, but it's not enough. Today's rapidly changing market and fast-paced world require all three. High-performance leaders will rise to the top and stay there by using their communication intelligence to Connect-Convey-Convince and change the world.

You can use the Connect-Convey-Convince method to successfully launch a career or a product, gain ground in your profession, win market share, or simply improve relationships.

Ask yourself, in the press of day-to-day activities, are you communicating in a way that engages people, helps them reach moments of clarity and true understanding, and encourages them to move quickly?

My hope is that you'll use these habits every day to meet today's communication challenges. If so, you'll be rewarded with quicker response times, more positive outcomes, and a boost in your personal ratings.

Less is truly more.

About the Author

Connie Dieken is the nation's leading authority on high performance communication in a short attention span world. The founder and president of onPoint Communication, she  helps leaders to speak as smart as they think and influence others to take positive action.

Organizations like Apple, Olympus, McDonald's, Moen, The Cleveland Clinic, Pacific Life, Progressive Insurance, and American Greetings turn to Connie to help them develop and deliver high-profile communications for winning outcomes at presentations, product launches, mergers and acquisitions, annual meetings, investor relations, culture shifts, media appearances, and leadership development. She helps them reach their highest performance in today's fast-paced, listening-impaired, shortcut society.

The country's foremost Fortune 500 communication coach, Connie is a former Emmy® Award-winning TV news anchor, reporter, talk show host, and inductee of the Radio/Television Broadcasters Hall of Fame. It was there, in television studios, where she discovered how leaders could capitalize on communication techniques to gain influence and improve business results. Since launching onPoint Communication, Connie has helped thousands of leaders achieve successful results. During the process, she earned a Leadership Think Tank

Award; the National Speakers Association's highest earned honor, the Certified Speaking Professional; and a NAWBO Top Ten Women Business Owners Award.

Connie has also coauthored four books: *Communicate Clearly, Confidently & Credibly* and the *303 Solutions* book series. She produced the innovative Connect-Convey-Convince communication method to improve business performance and her work has been featured in *The Los Angeles Times, Crain's Business, The Chicago Tribune, Women's Day,* and in dozens of other publications across the country.

Connie draws on her wealth of experiences in the ruthless world of broadcasting to fuel her research. Before launching onPoint, she spent more than twenty years as a television news anchor, reporter, and cohost of America's longest running television talk show, *The Morning Exchange.* She is a multiple Emmy® Award-winning and Telly® Award-winning journalist and has represented more than fifty companies as their spokesperson, including Intel, Sealy, GE, American Greetings, Ernst and Young, and Goodyear. She's also the voice of Diebold automated teller machines.

Connie delivers her insights through keynote addresses, coaching programs, leadership retreats, seminars, workshops, and strategic plans. She is a member of the National Speaker's Association, the National Association of Female Executives, and an active contributor to many charitable and civic projects.

Acknowledgments

This book is the result of more than twenty-five years of in-the-trenches research into how Communication Intelligence® improves performance and creates better business outcomes. My deepest thanks go to the thousands of businessmen and women who've shared their communication issues with me over the past decade at leading organizations such as Apple, Olympus, McDonald's, Moen, KraftMaid, Sterling Jewelers, The Cleveland Clinic, The Ohio State University, and Indiana University Kelley School of Business. The struggles and triumphs of business leaders in today's hectic workplaces have helped to shape and sharpen my Connect-Convey-Convince® communication methodology.

A special thanks goes to CEOs Bruce Carbonari of Fortune Brands, Tom Swidarski of Diebold, and David Lingafelter of Moen for endorsing this book. Many CEOs have allowed me to work closely with their executive teams and I am grateful for the experiences. Thank you for trusting me to help develop and improve the performance of leaders and emerging leaders within your world-class organizations.

I'd also like to express gratitude to my broadcast communication mentors from ABC Network News in New York, NBC-owned-and-operated WKYC in Cleveland, Ohio, WEWS-ABC in Cleveland, WSMV-NBC Nashville, and WTIU at Indiana University where I got my start. In addition, I want to recognize Karen King, my high school business teacher who, unbeknownst to me, signed me up for a national speaking contest that changed my life forever.

My thanks also go to my editor at John Wiley & Sons, Inc., Lauren Lynch, who guided me through the experience of publishing this book in half the time it traditionally takes to advance from manuscript to bookstores. You're reading this today because Lauren helped to move the process along efficiently and effectively.

Thanks to Lauren Freestone for guiding the production of *Talk Less, Say More* as well as designer Gwyn Kennedy Snider for her inspiration. In addition, my thanks to cover designer Michael J. Freeland and to designer Michele Monet, who has helped me communicate my ideas to audiences over the past decade and whose graphic images can be seen throughout this book. Thank you also to Jacqueline Frances Brownstein and Melanie Zimmerman for their sharp editing eye. All of these people inspire me and have elevated my ability to Connect-Convey-Convince® others to reach their highest performance.

I'd like to thank Sara Alvarado for helping to keep the onPoint office running smoothly as I was immersed in writing this book.

Also, my thanks to COSE Mindshare whose business owners read the manuscript and provided helpful feedback to make the content more valuable for you, the reader.

My loving gratitude belongs to my brother, Mike Schopmeyer, and my dad, Jim Alexander, for their many contributions to my communication adventures throughout the years.

Finally, to my lifeblood, my two children, Spencer and Ali, who inspired me to leave broadcasting and pursue my calling as an executive communication coach, author, and keynote speaker. They also encouraged me and waited patiently for their mother to finish chapters so they could eat, among other things. You make everything worthwhile, and I love you both with all my heart.

Index

Accordion structure, explained, 87
Alliteration, use of, 98
Amazon.com, 35, 85
American Idol, 14, 52
Analysis, insight versus, 33
Anger. *See* Difficult people
Anheuser-Busch, 71
Anxiety. *See* Stress
Apologizing
  admitting mistakes, 51
  guidelines for, 123–125
  tactical, 24–25, 26
Appearance, caveats, 81
Apple computer, 85, 110–112
Attention management. *See* Connecting
Austin, Dennis, 78

Berkshire Hathaway, 92, 97
Blogs
  and candor, 45
  to convey ideas, 80
  as tracking tool, 134
Body language
  power of, 78–79
  tips for using, 147–149
Branson, Richard, 144
Breathing, effective, 143, 149
Buffett, Warren, 92, 97, 144
Business-speak. *See* Jargon, caveats
Buy-in. *See* Convincing

Candor
  accepting criticism, 52–53
  action plan, 56–57
  culture of, 50–52
  demoralizing, 47–49
  power of, 43–47
  sugarcoating, 49–50
Charts, as visual aids, 75
Chat rooms, 134
Cheney, Dick, 145
Choices. *See* Options
Chrysler, 127
Clinton, Bill, 2, 139, 144–145
Clydesdale horses, 71
Cochran, Johnnie, 75–76
Code Red, 23–25
Columbia disaster, 46
Commitment. *See* Convincing
Communicating. *See* Conveying ideas
Communicators, influential. *See*
  Influencers
Communiclutter, 65–66

"Communi-fake," defined, 3
Compaq Center, 36
Comparisons, use of, 97–98
Confidence, expressing, 115–117
Connect-Convey-Convince®
  benefits, 2–3
  defined, 154–156
  evolution of, 1–2
Connecting
  action plan, 54–57
  attention management, 11–15
  candor, 43–53
  focus, 17–28
  frontloading, 29–41
  weakness in, 7–9
Contrast, as persuasion tool, 74–76
Contributors, as influencers,
  121–123
Conveying ideas
  action plan, 99–102
  information managment, 65–69
  storytelling, 91–98
  in triple bites, 83–89
  visually, 71–82
  weakness in, 61–63
Convincing
  action management, 109–114
  action plan, 150–153
  decisiveness factor, 115–125
  energy factor, 137–149
  ownership factor, 127–135
  weakness in, 105–107
Cramer, Jim, 137
Credibility
  damaging, 77–78, 121
  via decisiveness, 117
  projecting, 138–139
Criticism
  accepting, 26–27, 52–53
  excessive, 47–48, 52
Critiquing others, tips for, 27–28

Data dumping, 65–69
Decisiveness
  action plan, 150–151
  contributing and, 121–123
  hedging, 118–1120
  opinion-sharing tips, 123–125
  power of, 115–118
Defensiveness, defusing, 37–41. *See also*
  Difficult people
Demonstrations, as visual aids, 75
Demoralization, avoiding, 47–49